2nd edition

The Secret to Capitalizing on Analytics

A Web Analytics Approach for Beginners

By Tarek Riman

"How can you know where you are going if you don't know where you are?"

This book goes to my family, my friends, the hard-working entrepreneurs, the believers, the dreamers, the students and the fighters.

Never. Give. Up.

To God & The Universe *for blessing me with this journey, this book, and every breath.*

Published by
Cap.TaiM Marketing Inc.
captaim.com
ISBN: 9781796616194

Endorsements

"This is exactly the type of book that helps you understand the power of Analytics. It clearly demonstrates, with great examples, that Marketing success is not about what is measured but rather how and why one measures activities. This alone will help most Marketers effortlessly progress, at least 2/3 of the way, closer to their goals!"

Thomas Hormaza, Account Executive at The Weather Network – An Inspiring Marketer – AKA, the reason I ended up in marketing.

"Tarek has taught me a lot over the years & he's truly transferred his unparalleled analytical wisdom in this book. The Secret to Capitalizing on Analytics makes learning & setting up your analytics so simple!"

Adrian Salvadore, Digital Supervisor at Havas, Aspiring Digital Influencer

"A must-read for anyone new to analytics, digital marketing or data analysis. This book will show you how to get at the data you need, how to interpret it, and how to use it to drive intelligent business and marketing strategies in a digital world."

Melissa Dawn, Founder of CEO of Your Life

"An essential book to learn the basics of how to make the best use of your Analytics. In this book, Tarek manages to deconstruct the ever so daunting task of incorporating analytics into your business strategies in an easy to follow manner. This book can teach you how simple it can actually be and how best to use the advantages it provides."

Adriano Di Pancrazio, former student, aspiring copywriter, editor and digital marketer

Cover photos & Cover designed by Nancy Morris

Edits by Melissa Dawn, Erin Lariviere, and Shari Reinhart

DISCLAIMER

This book is designed to provide information, motivation and empowerment to readers. It is sold with the understanding that the author is not assured to deliver any kind of psychological advice (e.g. legal, medical, psychological) or be a substitute for professional assistance. No warranties or guarantees are expressed or implied by the writer in the content of this volume. The author shall not be liable for any physical, psychological, emotional, financial or commercial damages, including, but not limited to, special, incidental, consequential or other damages. The reader is responsible for their own choices, actions, and results. Situations, people and context have been changed as appropriate to protect the privacy of others.

Tarek Riman
Visit my website at www.captaim.com/book

Printed in the United States of America

First Printing: March 2019
Cap.TaiM Marketing Inc.

ISBN: 9781796616194

A Quick Introduction

The purpose of *The Secret to Capitalizing on Analytics* is to help start-ups, students, beginners and entrepreneurs understand how to use data and analytics to optimize and improve their business and marketing strategies.

All businesses today, no matter their size, should know how their website is performing. Without analytics, there is no way for a company to gauge their website's success (or lack thereof) in terms of attracting, informing and converting visitors, making it impossible to intelligently adapt, modify, improve and continually take your online presence to the next level.

In this book, you will learn how to get started with Google Analytics - the most powerful, complete and accessible analytics tool on the market today - and how to set it up for optimal tracking, reporting and testing. You will also learn how to assess which of your marketing campaigns and other external efforts bring the best traffic to your website, which pages on your website are the most popular, and how to extract information about your visitors. Specific details such as location, interests, age, behaviours and more, so that you can better understand your web traffic in order to capitalize on your marketing. You will also learn how to capitalize on the different trends and tools that are available today.

TABLE OF CONTENTS

Introduction

Analytics and Data Lessons for Everyone

Let's be honest, most entrepreneurs and small business owners want to get the best results possible, with as little monetary investment as possible. It sounds like having your cake and eating it too, but with a bit of time and know-how, you really can achieve Fortune 500 results, without the Fortune 500 budget.

Every time I stand in front of a conference audience, workshop group, or classroom of students eager to learn about digital marketing, I start off by saying this:

"We are not here to implement. We are not here to be the doers. We are not here to just receive the orders".

Many of you are probably familiar with the saying, "The numbers don't lie", but few people grasp the real significance. Numbers are the raw data collected. As such, they don't come with opinions, assumptions or bias. We add that after the fact. People are entitled to make their own assumptions and will bring their own interpretations to the data, but the numbers are what they are. From a digital marketing perspective, we can believe what we want about what will work, what our audience wants, and how they will interact with our site, but the numbers will hold the truth.

As you read this book, I want you to look beyond sites, apps and tracking.

My goal is that, by the end of this book, you won't only know how to use, implement and read data, but will also fall in love with data. Data is our foundation and our guide in all that we do. If you do the work to understand it, it can become your greatest ally.

I'm going to guide you through an elaborate (but accessible) tour. We're going up above this oversaturated subject to take a 360° view and break it down. What works for others doesn't mean it's going to work for you because every business and every owner has their own DNA and their own data. You need to concentrate on your values, get clear on your objectives and align with them, while paying attention to the numbers, the data and the logical aspects of what makes a business and a site work. This is exactly what we're going to do, go beyond basic marketing. Because if you want to stand out in this crowded space, this is the wide view that you have to take.

The Vision Behind the Book

To help, inspire, motivate and support. As I travel and work, I encounter a lot of people around the world who are struggling with over-complicated marketing ideas.

The goal of this book is to make sure that any business owner, student or marketer that picks up this book can immediately familiarize themselves with the concepts and begin using them to their advantage.

Disclaimer

In this book, as in life, there are no guarantees.

As the title indicates, this book is for beginners. It is intended to help them easily understand and capitalize on data and analytics to bring their brands to the next level.

Its purpose is to help you get started on web analytics and data, and to guide you to an understanding of how you can use them to your advantage in digital marketing.

The majority of the profits from this book will go to support refugees, education and child-related charities.

To stay posted on which charities we will be supporting, please visit our website: https://captaim.com/analytics-book

Glossary

Definition of Terms related to Web Analytics

Glossary of Terms

A/B test - An experiment that compares two or more versions of the same web page to see which one performs best. Also known as a split test or bucket test.

A/B/n test - Alternative name for A/B test to clarify that such tests can compare more than two versions of a web page.

Acquisition - The procurement of new visitors or users.

Actionable insight - Any insight upon which you can take action. This is one of the main purposes of analytics - to extract insight or knowledge that you can then act on to improve your business or marketing efforts.

Analytics - Analytics is the link between raw data and data-driven decision making. It is the process of aggregating, displaying and communicating data in a way that reveals meaningful patterns, with the intention of using those patterns to make stronger, knowledge-based decisions for your business.

Attribution model - A model for attributing credit for an acquisition, conversion or event on a web property.

Average position - The average position of your web property in search engine results pages (see SERP).

Behaviours - The actions people take on your web property, or on the internet in general. A behaviour can be scrolling, clicking, searching, entering information, watching a video, navigating to various pages, etc. It is how people interact with the internet or your web property.

Behavioural marketing - The process of marketing to specific behaviours. In this type of marketing, rather than deliver the same message or content to all users, you tailor content to specific behaviours. For example, you may create specific content for certain search terms, for return visitors, for shoppers who have items in their cart but have not checked out, etc.

Bid - In Google AdWords and other paid search platforms, businesses bid on their preferred keywords and search terms. The platform algorithm takes those bids into account in determining which ads are shown when, to whom and how often.

Blogging platform - A service used for blogging. Examples include WordPress and Tumblr.

Bounce - When a visitor to your web property leaves the site without ever taking any action.

Brand awareness - The level of audience recognition of your brand name, logo, tagline or other brand-specific elements. It can also refer to the likelihood that someone will think of your brand when faced with the problems you solve or gaps you fill in their daily life.

Branded term - A search term that includes the name of your brand or business.

Call to action (CTA) - A direction or invitation to site visitors to take a specific action. Examples include: buy now, sign up here, reserve your spot, download your free ebook, watch this video, etc.

Campaign - Coordinated activities with a specific objective to reach. From a marketing perspective, you may coordinate campaigns to boost sales during peak seasons, to build brand awareness, to collect newsletter subscribers, to promote specific products or services, etc.

Channels - Essentially, a pathway. For the purposes of this book, a channel can be the pathway taken by customers to get to your website (clicking on an ad or search result can be a channel), or it can be the pathway through which you promote your products or services (newsletters, ads, social media, etc.).

Click - When a user or visitor clicks on something. Depending on what you are tracking, this can be a click on a paid ad, a link on social media, an email or newsletter click, a click on a link within your site, etc.

Click through rate - The ratio of people who click a link over the number of people who view the page, ad, email, etc. For example, if 1,000 people see your AdWords ad and 10 of those people click on the ad, you would calculate 10/1,000x100 = 1, giving you a 1% click-through rate.

Content - Content is everything your visitors see or hear. Content can be copy, video, audio and images. Even quizzes or questionnaires can be considered content. It is what you put out there for your audience to consume.

Copy - Written words. Your copy is the text on your website, blog, newsletters, etc.

Container - From a software perspective, a container is much like a physical container in that it is meant to hold things. In this case, they are digital holders for code. Software code, and all of its dependencies, gets packaged up into a neat and tidy container, making it easier to move that code around and use it in different places, ensuring it runs reliably, since it has all its dependencies packaged up with it.

Conversion - A conversion is anytime a customer or site visitors complete a desired action on your web property. Conversions will differ from business to business, depending on your unique goals and objectives. Examples of conversions include a sale, newsletter sign up, app download, event registration, etc. The action must be fully completed to be considered a conversion.

Conversion rate - The percentage of visitors to your site or web property who complete a specific goal or objective. See "Conversion" above.

Creative - Another word for the graphic imagery used in marketing or advertising. The visual element of a newsletter, for example, may be referred to as the "creative".

Dashboard - A user interface that displays the most important information in a quick, easy-to-read fashion. An analytics dashboard, for example, is ideally laid out to show you your most critical stats and trends, immediately. Deep dives into data take place beyond the dashboard.

Data - In Google Analytics, data is the collected statistics and facts about your website or web properties, user behaviour and demographics, market trends, etc. It is raw information. On its own, it is simply too much information for humans to identify meaningful patterns and trends. Analytics is the organization of that data into something meaningful and readable. See "Analytics" above.

Data-driven strategy - Marketing or business strategies are driven by data. For example, instead of assuming that holidays will mean a boost in sales, we look to the data to see exactly when traffic, search or interest begins to rise, what specific terms are being used, who our audience is, etc., then we build marketing strategies off of that knowledge and insight.

Data hygiene - The practice of ensuring data is as "clean" as possible, meaning we are not collecting duplicate data, incomplete data, outdated data or otherwise compromised data. From a dashboard and reporting perspective, it is the practice of ensuring your visual data is clutter-free and easy to read. See "Dashboard" above.

Data mining - The practice of digging through large chunks of data to identify meaningful patterns or trends. With the massive amounts of data today's technology gives us access to, data mining can typically only be done by machines.

Data source - The source of your information. For example, if you have connected Google Analytics and Google Ads, when you view data from AdWords within Analytics, AdWords is your data source.

Demographics - Population-based factors such as geographical location, age, language, gender, religion, education, etc.

Device - The physical product used by someone to access your site or web property. Examples of devices include laptop or desktop computers, smartphones and tablets.

Digital marketing - All marketing conducted and consumed in the digital realm.

Dimensions - In Google Analytics, dimensions are the data attributes. For example, if you are looking at the number of page views for a specific page, "page views" would be your dimension, the number of page views would be your metric. See "Metrics" below.

Ecommerce - The practice of selling products or services online. An eCommerce site is a site that sells something.

Email marketing - The practice of promoting products or services, building brand awareness or conducting any other marketing activity through email. Typically, email newsletter subscribers are gathered through online forms, at points of sale, or some other method of email collection. However, emails such as registration confirmations, order receipts, etc. can sometimes include marketing elements and, therefore, fall under the umbrella of "email marketing".

Engagement - When a brand and consumer connect in a meaningful way. Engagement on a website is often measured by time spent on site, or the number of actions taken on a site. It is when a visitor discovers content that holds their attention and keeps them interested.

Event - Any action taken on a site or web property. This can be a click, playing a video, downloading content, sharing on social media, etc.

Exit - When someone leaves your site or web property. They may close the app or web browser, or leave to go to another site.

External site - This usually refers to linking. When another website (for example, a blog or online magazine) links to your website, you would say the traffic from that link is coming from an external site. Essentially, it is any website outside of your network.

Funnel - The pathways visitors take to get to a desired location. For example, if visitors typically start on your homepage, navigate to a Services page, then navigate to a Contact Us page, that journey would be your typical visitor funnel. Funnels get more complex the more pages you have on your site. Ecommerce sites, for example, can have very complex funnels. Insight into these funnels help us identify where we may be losing people so that we can improve the funnel to increase conversions.

GDPR (General Data Protection Regulation) - Regulation adopted by the EU concerning data privacy. The regulation applies to businesses located outside the EU as well, if they intend to do business within the EU. To learn more, visit www.gdpr.associates.

Gmail - Google's free email service. To use any Google service, you first need a Gmail account.

Goals - In Google Analytics, a goal is an action you want visitors to complete. It can be a completed sale or sign up, a specific page destination, an amount of time spent on the site, etc.

Google Analytics - Web analytics service that tracks website or mobile app traffic and behaviour, and presents it in a readable report format.

Google Analytics Demo Account - A demo account supported by Google for beginners to learn how to use Google Analytics, or for seasoned users to get familiar with different features and options before trying them out in the real world.

Google AdWords - Online advertising platform where advertisers bid on keywords and phrases to have their ads displayed alongside search results and websites within the Google advertising network.

Google Data Studio - Google Data Studio is all about the aesthetics of reporting. It allows you to create reports and dashboards that are easy to read and easy to understand. You can also add branding and other personalization elements to reports in GDS.

Google Insights - A Google service that provides insight into people's search behaviour and preferences. It does not provide any personally identifiable information. Instead, it shows search trends by date, geographical location and demographic information.

Google Optimize - A Google tool that allows you to run tests on your website, emails, app or other digital properties to determine the best performing elements.

Google Search Console - This tool allows you to see how your site is performing from a search perspective. What keywords are people using to find you? Where is your site showing up in search results pages? How often are people clicking on your search results? You can find all that through GSC.

Google Tag Manager - This tool allows you to create and manage tags (See "Tags" below). A tag could be the GA code embedded on your site, or the UTM tags (See "UTM tag" below) you use to track campaigns. You manage all of those tags from within GTM.

Google Trends - This tool gives you insight into search trends. You can use it to identify seasonal spikes or slumps in searches for your brand, related brands, your products or services, etc.

Implementation - From a marketing perspective, implementation is the process of actually putting a marketing campaign live and into action. It is the actual sending of newsletters, putting new content live, posting to social media, etc.

Impressions - Anytime your content is displayed on a screen. This could be a webpage, an ad, an embedded video, etc. Each display of the content is considered an impression.

Intent - In marketing, when we talk about intent, we're talking about the user's intention when they take an action. For example, if someone looks up "dry cleaner" in a Google search, their intention is most likely to find dry cleaning services near them. They probably aren't looking for the dictionary definition of "dry cleaner" or the history of dry cleaning. Intent matters because giving people what they want is how businesses thrive.

Keywords - The words and phrases people enter into search engines when looking for products, services, information, etc.

Landing page - The specific page a visitor lands on when they first arrive at your site. For example, if someone on your company Facebook page clicks a link to your latest blog post, the blog post they arrive at is their landing page.

Leads - A lead is collected contact information of someone who is not yet a customer, but may become one. A newsletter subscriber is one example. This person has not yet purchased from you, but you now have their email address and permission to contact them, which you can then use to market products and services in hopes of converting them to a customer.

Link-building - When evaluating the quality and/or relevancy of a website, one of the things search engines take into account is the external site (See "External site" above) linking to yours. Having several links from other reputable sites that are directed to your site, boosts the validity of your site in the eyes of search engines. Link building is the practice of actively seeking out external links to your site. One common way of doing this is by providing content (articles, videos, etc.) to external blogs or online magazines that link back to your website. It can be a time consuming and lengthy process, and takes dedication, but the payoff is big. Not only do search engines see these links favourably, but they also increase brand awareness and often send high-quality traffic your way.

Load time - The time it takes for all elements of a webpage to be fully displayed.

Local marketing - There are two types of local marketing. If you are a local business, you will focus your marketing on your immediate location. You wouldn't spend resources getting your brand in front of audiences that are nowhere near you. The other type is when you customize your marketing based on where it will be seen, geographically. An eCommerce site, for example, may customize the products they market based on the interests or seasons of particular regions instead of showing the exact same content everywhere.

Macro conversion - Any conversion that your business deems as most important. See "Conversion" above.

Marketing strategy - A business's overall approach to marketing its products or services.

Measurement - The practice of measuring the results of campaigns or the performance of a web property.

Medium - The singular of "media". In marketing, a medium is typically a single source. For example, all social networks fall under the umbrella of "social media", but one specific network, such as Facebook or LinkedIn, would be considered a social medium.

Messaging - The words you use to talk about and promote your brand or business. A best practice for building solid brand awareness is to establish a clear, compelling message and to be consistent in using only that messaging.

Metadata - The data about your data. Examples include page titles, file names, image titles, etc.

Metrics - A quantifiable measurement of a dimension. For example, if you are looking at total impressions, "impression" is your dimension, and the total number is your metric. See "Dimensions" above.

Micro conversion - A minor, less valuable conversion. For example, your business's most important goal may be sales, but you may also have a newsletter for which you collect subscribers. In that case, you may consider a newsletter subscription to be a micro-conversion, while a sale is a macro conversion. See "Conversion" and "Macro conversion" above.

Mobile - Mobile devices, such as tablets or smartphones.

Mobile site - The version of your website that is adapted for mobile devices.

Multivariate test - A test of multiple elements within a webpage. Multivariate tests can be incredibly granular and incredibly insightful. For example, you may test the elements of a single button: button text, button colour, font, rounded corners vs. square, etc.

Non-PII data - Non Personally Identifiable Information Data. This is the type of data you will find in Google Analytics. It can give you the metrics of a visitor age range, geographical location, gender, etc., but it does not provide any information that can be used to identify a particular individual.

Optimization - The practice of using every resource and insight available to you to improve your web properties, marketing strategies, etc. in order to increase business success.

Organic search - Also called natural search. When a search engine user types in a search term, the non-paid generated results are considered organic search. They are the result of search engine spiders crawling the web to gather data and the search engine algorithms determining which results best match the user's search terms and other demographic information. See "Paid search" below.

Page extension - The part of a URL that comes after the main domain name. For example, www.google.com would be the main domain name. In the case of www.google.com/maps, the /maps part of the URL is called the page extension.

Paid search - The practice of paying to have your business's ad appear on search engine results pages when users search for certain keywords or phrases.

Persona - A profile of your target audience. In marketing, it can help with creating truly engaging and authentic content to imagine creating it for a specific individual. This can also help you in targeting that content effectively. Typically, you would want to have several personas, depending on the demographics of your typical customer(s) or target customer(s).

Property (in GA) - A web-based property for which you (or your company) are the owner. This may be a website, a mobile app, a community forum, etc., but it must be solely owned by you (or your business). A social network profile like LinkedIn, for example, is technically owned by the social network; therefore, it would not be considered a property.

Query - A query is essentially a question to be answered. When a search engine user types in their search terms, that is one example of a query. When you create a report in GA with filters, that is also a query.

Rank - In marketing, rank typically refers to where your business listing shows up in organic search results for particular keywords or phrases. For example, if you are a Montreal-based bicycle store and your listing shows up in fourth place when someone searches for "Montreal bike shops", you have a ranking of 4. See "Organic search" above.

Real-time - At this exact moment. For example, when you view the real-time report in Google Analytics, you are seeing the activity taking place on your web property at this exact moment.

Redirect test - This is when you want to compare the performance of different landing pages. An example of a redirect test may be to send an email newsletter to your full subscriber list with a link to "shop now". Your list would be randomly split in two and clicking the "shop now" link would redirect them to either the specific product page or to the product department page to see which one performs best in generating sales.

Remarketing - The practice of targeting ads to people who have visited your web property but did not make a purchase or otherwise convert (See "Conversion" above). If you have ever visited a website and left without purchasing, then started seeing ads for that site pop up in your social networks and search listings, that's remarketing.

Return on investment (ROI) - The monetary return generated from investing in a marketing campaign or other effort to increase sales. Obviously, you want your return to be greater than what you put in. Ideally much greater.

Search engine - A web service used to search for products, services or other information on the web. Examples include Google, Bing and Yahoo.

Search engine marketing (SEM) - The practice of increasing your website's visibility in search engine results. Typically, this is done by paying for ad listings. See "Paid search" above.

Search engine optimization (SEO) - The practice of optimizing your website structure, content and linking (See "Link building" above) in order to increase your website's visibility in organic search results (See "Organic search" above).

Search engine results page (SERP) - The page of results shown after a search engine user types in their search query.

Search performance - The performance of your web property in organic search results. See "Organic search" and "Rank" above.

Search ranking - The ranking of your web property in organic search results. See "Organic search" and "Rank" above.

Search term - The terms entered into a search engine by a user in order to find specific products, services or other information.

Session - The duration of a visitor's entire visit, from the moment they land on your website or property, until they leave.

Site search - Search capabilities embedded within a website. Whenever you visit a website and are able to search within that site using an embedded search tool, that's site search.

Site speed - The speed with which a site loads pages and page elements.

Site structure - Refers to how the pages within your site are linked together both visually and in the background. This matters from a user experience perspective (how easily people are able to find things and navigate your site) and a search perspective (how easily search engines are able to find the content on your site). This is especially important for websites that have many pages, such as eCommerce sites or online magazines.

Sitelink - These are the links that sometimes appear under a search result in a search engine results page (See "Search engine results page' above). They typically link to subpages within the main website.

Social media - Any platform or tool through which users are able to engage socially with each other. For example, Facebook, LinkedIn, Twitter and Instagram are all examples of social media, but a comments section or forum may also be considered a form of social media.

Social media marketing - Any type of marketing carried out through social media. Maintaining a Facebook business page, for example, is a form of social media marketing.

Tags - A tag is a form of metadata (See "Metadata" above). It is information about information. For example, when you tag someone in a picture on Facebook, you are providing information (a person's identity) about information (the picture). From a software perspective, a tag is used to provide information about the information within the site code.

Target market - The set of demographic data you want to target in your marketing efforts is your target market. For example, you may be targeting millennials of a particular income bracket living in a certain geographical area. A target market can also be campaign based. For example, an eCommerce site like Amazon sells a range of products that cater to just about anyone on Earth. Instead of marketing to the entire world, they create specific target markets to market to (See also "Persona" above).

Tracking code - The snippets of code used to track pages, links or entire websites for analytics purposes.

Traditional marketing - Marketing that takes place outside the digital realm. Television commercials (even though most TVs are digital today, commercials existed pre-digital), magazine advertorials, direct mailings, etc. are all examples of traditional marketing.

Traffic - The flow of visitors to your website or web property.

Traffic sources - Where your visitors come from. They may be coming from search engines, social media, blogs, online articles, email newsletters, etc.

Trend - A pattern. From a digital marketing perspective, we examine data to identify trends or patterns in things like visits, sales, clicks, etc. in order to capitalize on them.

Trend measurement - The practice of measuring trends in the market.

Urchin - Urchin Software Corporation was a web analytics company that was acquired by Google in 2005. Its software forms the foundation of Google Analytics.

User - A person interacting with a site or web property.

User driven metrics - Metrics based on user behaviour (See "Metrics" and "User" above). Examples of user driven metrics include average time on site, bounce rate, pages per visit, etc.

User experience - The experience a visitor has when interacting with your site or web property. This includes load time, site structure, general functionality, level of engagement with content, etc. (See "Content", "Engagement", "Load time" and "Site structure" above).

User flow - The steps a user must take to complete a conversion or other goal.

UTM tag - Urchin Tracking Module (See "Urchin" above). A UTM tag is a snippet of code added to the end of a URL for tracking purposes. This allows you to track specific campaigns (specific newsletters or ads, for example) or traffic sources (social networks or blog posts, for example).

View (in GA) - These are your reports. It is your "view" into specific queries into your data. See "Query" above.

Visitors - The people visiting your site or web property.

Web property - A web-based property for which you (or your company) are the owner. This may be a website, a mobile app, a community forum, etc., but it must be solely owned by you (or your business). A social network profile like LinkedIn, for example, is technically owned by the social network; therefore, it would not be considered a property.

Word of mouth - A form of marketing and/or lead and sales acquisition that relies on users or customers telling their friends, family, colleagues, etc. about your business, product or service.

Analytics

Digital Marketing Analytics

Chapter 1.1- An Introduction

Data is power, especially in marketing.

When working towards any goal, it is critical to know exactly where you are, what's working, what isn't working, and what opportunities you have to grow and improve. That insight is how you drive progress, and you get that insight from the wealth of data that analytics can provide.

Ultimately, how we use this data depends on us. With time, our roles as marketers will become more about data and less about doing and creating, as the doing and creating will be driven by the data.

To succeed, to excel, to survive, you must become a master of analytics and grasp all that it has the power to do.

Learn it. Master it. Act on what it gives you. And, most of all, continue to evolve your own knowledge and skills alongside the continual evolution of the tools and technology. That's how you win.

Chapter 1.2 - Reasons to Master Google Analytics

How can business benefit from analytics?

Google Analytics, or, for those of us in the know, GA, tells you how your site is performing, right? It sure does. But it tells you a lot more than that. In fact, over the past few years, technical capabilities have advanced so much that the list of insights GA can provide is practically endless.

Where visitors come from, what they do on your site, end-to-end funnels, top-performing content, top supporting content, missed trend opportunities...the list goes on.

Yes, Google Analytics is a free tool. But this is one instance where "you get what you pay for" just doesn't hold up. Instead, this is a case of "you get what you put in."

Learn it. Master it. Put in the ongoing work. What you will get out of it is invaluable. If you need convincing, here are just five reasons to master GA:

1. **Your competitors will**
    The insights you can get out of GA are invaluable. It can identify untapped market demographics, off-season trends to capitalize on, upcoming search trends and more. Whether you decide to jump on that massive advantage or not, your competitors will (if they haven't already). Once they do, you don't want to be scrambling to catch up. Invest in mastery now, learn how to use the insights to strengthen your presence, and you will be well placed to get, or stay, on top.

2. **Turn your off-season into your hustle season**
    Virtually every business has an off or low season. Even Amazon sees dips outside of peak shopping times. But there are always opportunities to jump on, even if your product or service is seasonal. Whether it's branding or partnership opportunities to keep your name top-of-mind, or search rankings to strengthen so you're well positioned to absolutely nail your peak seasons, off-season is only "off" if you allow it. When you

master GA, off-season quickly becomes hustle season.

3. **It makes you desirable and hireable!**
   If you're a student, looking to change careers, or want to go for that big promotion, being a master of data and analytics is currently, and will continue to be, one of the most in-demand job market skills. At higher levels, mastering GA means you have the skillset to make data-driven decisions and design strategies based on hard data. At the entry-level, being a GA master means businesses will want you for your ability to build, generate and read an array of reports. That can be tedious work, which is why it's great for interns and entry-level employees, but because you learn so much about a business by studying reports, you are in the perfect position to get ahead.

4. **Become EXACTLY what your target market wants**
   You can conduct as many surveys and focus groups as your resources will allow, but nothing tells you what people truly want better than their actual, real-world behaviour. Now, let's be clear. GA doesn't give you personally identifiable information about any specific person. But, it can give you incredibly granular insights into specific groups, allowing you to understand how different demographic groups, traffic sources, device users, etc. actually behave online. What type of content they interact with and when. What they share, click, buy, search for. What grabs their attention, what loses their attention, and so much more. It empowers you in a way no technology or strategy in the past ever has.

5. **Create a data-driven marketing calendar**
   Like most businesses, you probably have a calendar of key holidays, seasons and events for creating targeted marketing campaigns. Great. But, do you know *for sure* that you're capitalizing on every potential event? Do you know *exactly* what terms people are using to search for products, services and other content around those events? Do you know *without a doubt* which of your content items has the highest conversion rate and how it performs best? GA will tell you that, and more, so you can build a strong, data-driven marketing calendar, modify it as needed to address changing market trends, and consistently stay ahead of the pack.

Chapter 1.3- The Importance of Analytics in Today's Market

Analytics and data matters now more than ever

Analytics Matters More Today Than Ever Before

I often say to my students, "A business without analytics is a blind business. After all, how can you know where you're going if you don't know where you are?"

To best predict your future, you need to have a really clear picture of your past and present.

Analytics: Past & Present

What once involved intense manual data mining, report creation, repetition and a whole lot of human error has become more and more automated as the years have progressed.

And, because machines tend to move faster than humans (certainly where data processing is concerned), the rate of change in the field of analytics has been getting faster and faster.

The existence of change has always been there (and always will be); it's just now happening at unprecedented speeds, with updates, upgrades and plenty more "ups" happening on a daily basis.

Marketing: Past & Present

When the speed of change in analytics increases, so too can the speed at which we adapt our marketing and business strategies. And that's a good thing.

Being able to make informed business decisions that are fully aligned with your dreams and objectives is a powerful thing. The more efficient analytics becomes, the more efficient we become at making those amazing decisions.

Your Business: Past & Present

I'm not clairvoyant, so I can only offer guidance, but let me ask you this: Are you investing ⅔ of your marketing efforts into analytics?

Looking towards future predictions, you may be surprised that trends show about ⅔ of all marketing is now, and will most likely continue to be, based strongly on analytics and data.

So, if you are spending the majority of your efforts on implementation, think twice.

Back to Marketing

Given the trends as of this book's writing, I see marketing summarised by three key pursuits: research, implementation and measurement.

Research and measurement both require a strong understanding of analytics. That's where the ⅔ value mentioned above comes from. These two pursuits are both heavily dependent on your understanding and use of analytics. They cannot happen, in a competitive way, without that analytics foundation. This is why I insist that the majority of your efforts should go towards analytics.

Additionally, as you likely already know, the value of analytics goes beyond marketing. It also plays a key role in other areas of business decision making. Therefore, making the investment on the marketing side will pay off beyond that.

Takeaway

Analytics goes beyond marketing.

From a business perspective, analytics is a goldmine. If you know how to mine it. Tap into the full benefits on analytics and think beyond just marketing.

Exercise:

Think about the different aspects of your business and write down the areas that you are least knowledgeable about - meaning, the areas for which you have the least amount of data. This could be lead generation, customer retention, website performance, traffic sources, campaign performance, search performance... consider all aspects.

Knowing where you need to have more data is the most important part of going after data. It empowers you to put the effort where the effort is needed most.

Chapter 1.4 - Why is Analytics Important for Businesses?

Analytics = Business knowledge, Strategy and Intelligence.

Analytics = business intelligence, and that's always a good thing. But there are other ways of gathering business intelligence. So why is analytics so important? Why is this now the gold standard for intelligence, insight and knowledge-based decision making? The numerous ways you can use analytics would be a whole other book on its own. For this book, I'll focus mainly on how analytics helps turn your website into a conversion-driving machine.

Here are just 5 of the reasons analytics is taking center stage:

1. Match the message to the traffic

Analytics gives insight into which type of traffic is most engaged with what type of content and who is most likely to buy your product or service.

By understanding your different audiences, you can create campaigns that target them with relevant content and aligned strategies, leading to higher conversions.

Essentially, you'll know who responds to what, taking a lot of guesswork out of implementation.

2. Understand how people navigate your site

It's important to know who your visitors are and, more important, to understand how they behave on your site.

Understanding how visitors engage with your web property shows you where they enter, what they interact with, where conversions originate and where people quit. Understanding specific user flows on your site empowers you to make changes that address your business goals, whether it's keeping people on your site longer, funnelling them to specific content, or taking specific actions.

3. Know your traffic sources

Simply put, when you know which sources drive the most (and best quality) traffic, you know exactly where to direct further investments of time, money and/or effort.

4. Get clear on the actual interests of people visiting your site

The better you know your clients and visitors, the better you can cater to their needs, the greater your business will grow.

Analytics gives insight into valuable demographics, which you can capitalize on. Those can include age, gender, interests, device type, location... it goes on.

Having access to this information helps you create more relevant personas and exceptional targeting.

5. Recycle your analytics in other business areas

The thing about information is that you can use it over and over again, for as many different purposes as you like.

The idea that analytics is only for analytics experts or marketing professionals is flat out wrong.

Knowledge empowers everyone. Circulate that knowledge throughout your organization so whether someone is working in customer service or product design, they have a wealth of information right at their fingertips to help make better business decisions.

Takeaway

Remember that, ultimately, it isn't about the information you get from analytics. It's about what you do with it. Invest in bringing that critical knowledge and insight into your business, then use it!

Chapter 1.5 - Analytics and Behaviours

Change is the Only Constant

Change is the Only Constant

Consumers are not static groups.

Your consumers are not one dimensional. For marketers, they are a dynamic collection of varying behaviours. Essentially, we're shooting at moving targets. And, in a moving target scenario, intelligence into your target's behaviour is invaluable. The insight we can get into those behaviours is immense.

Market to Behaviours

We are no longer marketing to consumers.

Marketing is a constantly shifting landscape. What we do today -- what we *can* do today -- would have been unimaginable to most people just ten years ago. And, what we will be able to do ten years from now, will go beyond what we can imagine with the digital marketing capabilities we have today. Use what is available now.

The technology available today means there is so much more we are capable of doing. To be successful, you have to do it. Once upon a time, Henry Ford's idea was to make one good car in one colour. It worked then. But that strategy won't sell cars today. Cars have changed. Consumers have changed. The world has changed.

A decade ago, word of mouth marketing was the big buzz. Even that has evolved. Today we still have word-of-mouth marketing, but it's supported with a plethora of tools to broadcast it, giving consumers not just control over messaging, but over distribution as well.

We have arrived at a point in history where nearly everyone is broadcasting their every experience in some way. We are constantly feeding into our various devices, and they are feeding off of us. Smart devices have spread across nearly every culture and household.

We are, as a people, more tech-savvy and more connected than ever before. And yet, also more concerned with our privacy than ever before.

Just when we think we've mastered the art of social media and digital marketing, the game changes. Who is the real master of the game? Are we, as marketers, in charge? Or are consumers leading the way? If the consumer is in charge, who are we marketing to? Is marketing static?

The answer is, we are no longer marketing to consumers. We are marketing to behaviours.

Marketing to behaviours means marketing to a series of emotions, demands, habits, visits and more. No other type of marketing gives such a full picture of your customer. Who is he? What does she like? What does he buy? Who does she interact with?

It is the collective information of these diverse moving targets of variables that we strive to attain, interpret and act on. It is the full use of all real-time data while cross-referencing it with RTB (real-time bidding) and programmatic ad-buying (don't worry if that went over your head - we'll get more into that further along).

The ads, copy, displays and all creative we generate is with a specific behaviour or set of behaviours in mind. We attempt to predict them, understand them and influence them.

For marketing purposes, behaviours are the collection of data from a consumer's everyday life. We currently collect information from consumers every minute of every day. In the past, we relied on surveys and feedback to gather that data, which was hardly accurate. What a consumer said they did or liked in a survey could be vastly different from their actual, real-life behaviours. Today, we gather data from the source. We can track and interpret actual behaviour and patterns in real life and in real-time.

A behaviour is a collection of:

Social Inputs:

- Likes
- Dislikes
- Favourites
- Follows
- Unfollows
- Comments
- Tweets and retweets
- Video views
- Podcast streams
- Pages
- Shares
- Chats
- Messages
- Pictures
- Sites and web properties
- Visits
- Time spent on a site
- Bounces
- Sources of traffic

Subscriptions and feeds:
- Email sign-ups
- Site registrations
- Feeds/RSS

Conversions and traffic flow:
- Attributions and attribution modelling
- Interests, browser preference and language tracking

Does that sound like an overwhelming number of variables to consider? In the past, it would have been. Today, all of this data is right at your fingertips via tools and sources like Google Analytics, Google Insights, Facebook Insights, Twitter Analytics, Web Trends and Google Trends.

How do we use this data in the real world? Let's take a look at the headphone industry for an example of how a good marketer can capitalize on behaviour and insights using data.

The graph below, gathered from Google Trends, shows the North American market interest associated with both headphones and gifts.

Blue: Gifts

Red: Headphones

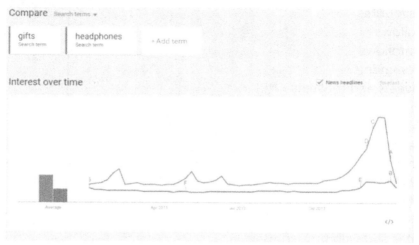

What the data shows is that the largest jump in market interest in gifts is during the winter holiday season. That's not surprising, but what a good marketer will realize is that there are three additional gift-giving periods they may not have been taking advantage of throughout the year.

Looking closely at gift search interest from February to July, you can see the three additional peaks: Valentine's Day, Mother's Day and Father's Day.

After seeing this data, an insightful and behaviour-driven approach would be to launch three different paid search and content campaigns targeting people searching for gifts around these dates, with these specific interests in mind. That will also help change the trend in the coming years and yield more growth. Gathering, analyzing and acting on the available data enables marketers to add three additional high yield campaigns to the annual marketing calendar.

For some companies, they have not yet put in place the tools to use this data effectively. Some collect monthly data and act accordingly. Others look at annual data trends and modify next year's strategies based on what they see. This is not a winning game plan. For that reason, we've seen a huge turnover in Fortune 500s and Fortune 1000s. The list has changed considerably in the last five years. What's happening to those businesses that drop off? Much of it comes down to how quickly they respond to market changes.

It's time to innovate. It's time to become masters of the data we have. It's time for businesses to evolve and react as quickly as consumers in order to provide a better experience and build better businesses.

These tools are there for us to create effective campaigns and achieve higher ROIs on the whole.

Let's use the incredible technology we have at our fingertips and use it to its fullest capacity. Let's reach the hearts and minds of consumers as we've never reached them before. Let's be active in the evolution of our markets and audiences. Let's become the masters of behavioural marketing.

Takeaway

What many marketers fail to understand is that analytics and data are 2/3 of a truly successful marketing journey.

As a marketer, invest your time accordingly. Don't drain your resources on implementation and doing. Put it into intelligence, and your implementation will be far more successful.

Exercise:

Go to Google Trends - https://trends.google.com/trends/ - and input some of the terms that relate to your business. Try to identify and understand the similarities and correlations in the trends.

Once you have found a connection, you can use this data to better align your business and marketing strategies with what the market is really about. In this way, your efforts become intelligence-driven, rather than based on theory or speculation.

Chapter 1.6 - The Method
Try, Measure, Analyze and Update

Marketing has always been about trying. Trying new approaches, new tricks, new creatives, new algorithms, etc. A great marketer knows that there is no magic trick; no ideal formula. A great marketer makes many mistakes but always learns from them.

Your off-season is a great time to test, measure, update and prepare the ideal marketing mix for your high seasons. When your high season comes around, you can focus all your efforts on capitalizing on the busy period without needing to try out new (and potentially ineffective) marketing strategies. Testing could be as simple as splitting your email newsletter list to test two different subject lines, calls to action, graphics or any other element, then measuring and comparing the results from each test. Google even has tools that allow you to test multiple web pages, so you can test variations of your homepage or a new landing page.

Your tests don't have to be complicated or costly. In fact, the most insightful tests are the simplest, focusing on one element at a time. If you test two completely different landing pages, for example, you won't know which element was ultimately the "success" element. But let's say the two pages are identical except for a different button colour, or different text on that button or one page gets a button, the other gets a text link. Then you get a clearer picture of what your visitors respond to, and you can grow from there.

The key is to accept that this is not a one-and-done scenario. Change is constant. The only way we can stay ahead of the game is by continuously trying, measuring, analyzing and updating. I wish the anagram were catchier, but in this case, clarity wins over flash. Let's explore TMAU!

Trying

Trying is all about testing ideas, trying new strategies, and continually striving to take your efforts to the next level. The market is constantly changing, meaning you need to be prepared to change with it. Don't wait for things to stop working before you figure out why. Keep testing.

Measuring

Plan your tests with measurement in mind. As Peter Drucker said, "What gets measured gets managed." If you're testing multiple elements, know ahead of time exactly how each element will be measured and how the data will be collected.

Analyzing

Also, plan your tests with analysis in mind. How will you analyze the data that comes in? How will the different data sets be compared? What format do you need them to analyze effectively? With Google Analytics, you have multiple report options within the tool. Those reports can be downloaded if needed, as can your raw data. Most analytics tools offer that, but some may not, and some have limited reporting options. Make sure you know you can get your data in a format that can be efficiently analyzed. Remember, if you can't understand the data, it isn't useful.

Updating

There are two parts to updating:

1. Update your website, newsletter, strategy, business practices, or whatever it is you're testing based on the results of the tests. Analytics is about understanding the data and USING it. Why go to all the effort of trying, analyzing and measuring if you aren't going to do anything about it?

2. Update your tests! There's always another level to get to, another market shift to get ahead of, another opportunity to take advantage of, another competitor on your heels. Don't think of progress as a noun. It's a verb. It's active. Keep doing it. Keep progressing. Still, waters get stagnant. Rivers go places. Be the river.

Takeaway

Remember that just because a strategy is free or low cost does not mean it's less effective. Often, it's not about the money you put in, but the effort you put in.

Trying, measuring, analyzing and updating is a strategy already being used by many Fortune 500 companies to drive big results. You don't need a big budget to see big results for your business too. You do need commitment, consistency and the drive to keep progressing.

Chapter 1.7. - Important Web Trends and Analytics Tools

Use Trend Measurement Tools

3 Trend Measurement Tools Your Business Needs

Wouldn't it be great to have the inside track on the next big thing? Or insight into what's going to grab your market's attention? Once you knew that, the question would be how to capitalize on that insight.

Trend management tools can be a bit like crystal balls but based on data, not fantasy. Beyond insight into the future, they also help you plan for the future. As entrepreneurs, we all want to predict the future. In the past, we used historical data and, essentially, educated guessing to determine future trends. That left a large margin for error and, with today's faster pace of change, historical data isn't always a reliable predictor of the future.

Trend measurement tools are making future predictions much more accurate, because they use real-time data input, and can aggregate data from multiple sources, across multiple platforms and enable you to quickly analyze, compare and understand the data in many different ways. These tools really do give you an edge in the market.

There are four key factors that make trend measurement tools vital to success:

1. Understanding trends empowers you to leverage every growth opportunity and each moment your competition might be missing.

2. Trends help you prepare for downturns. Knowing about a market slump in advance lets you better prepare for it, which can be just as valuable as being able to capitalize on upturns.

3. Trends give you insight into how often people search for your brand vs competitors, so you can understand the lows and highs of the competition and plan accordingly.

4. Trends provide insight into your industry overall. If you're just starting a business, this helps you enter the market strategically. If you're up and running, it enables you to tailor content to your market and adjust that content as the market changes.

5. So, what trend management tools will give you what you need? Once again, Google is the frontrunner, with three powerful (and free, at least as of this writing) tools that can be used for trend management. **The Best (Free) Tools**

Tool #1 - Google Trends

Let's go back to that headphone example from earlier in the book. Imagine you are a headphones company and want to capitalize on peak interest throughout the year.

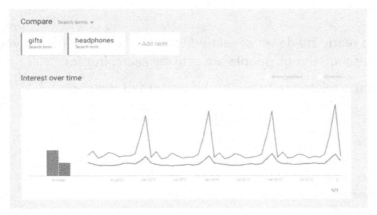

Google Trends shows you a year over year trend for the term "gifts" and a similar trend for "headphones", co-occurring during the December/January holiday period.

However, as we saw earlier, there are also three additional opportunities around Valentine's Day, Father's Day and Mother's Day.

Once we have that insight, we can act accordingly to capitalize on these untapped market trends. An example could be, "An Unconventional Gift for an Unconventional Dad".

Tool #2 – Google

Start typing in Google. What do you see? A bunch of autocomplete suggestions and related topics. Helpful when you're looking for something…. SUPER helpful to know what others are looking for! Although this is more of a feature than a standalone tool, there is a wealth of insight to be gleaned from the results.

Here's an example:

You are a real estate start-up running out of blog ideas. You need to fill up your editorial calendar.

Type "5 things to consider before moving out" into Google. It's a broad topic and hard to rank on for SEO, but related topics have more potential.

Take a look at the autocomplete suggestions:

It's not only a ready-made list of related topics to write about, but you now know that these are things people are actively searching for.

Next, look at the related searches at the bottom of the page:

Searches related to 5 things to consider before moving out

things to consider before moving in with someone

things to consider before moving in together

things to consider before moving in with boyfriend

things to consider before moving in with your boyfriend

things to consider before moving to a new city

things to consider when moving out on your own

things to consider when moving out for the first time

things to consider when moving out of state

Yet another ready-made list to inspire blog posts, articles, newsletters and much more. And again, since these results are driven by what other people are searching for, if you build content around them, you know you're creating something that provides real value. This is far more than guessing or taking a shot in the dark. This is data-driven strategy.

Tool #3 - Google AdWords/Google Ads

What? AdWords isn't free! Well, you do have to pay for ads, but an AdWords account is free and comes with the handy (and free) Keyword Tool, which finds related trends and measures their search volume. With a free AdWords account, you get full access to this tool and its powerful features.

Keyword	Avg. Monthly Se:	Competition
things to consider when moving out of state	110	0.22
things to consider before moving in together	**90**	**0.01**
things to consider before moving in with your boyfriend	40	0
things to consider when moving out for the first time	**30**	**0.02**
things to consider before moving in with someone		
things to consider before moving in with boyfriend		
things to consider before moving to a new city		
things to consider when moving out on your own		

Using terms from our real estate example, you can see that the first 4 topics are most worth writing about, based on average monthly searches.

But take a look at the second column - Competition. AdWords operates on a bidding model, with advertisers bidding on different keywords and phrases to get their ads displayed. The Competition column you see above indicates the level of competitiveness for each phrase, giving you an idea of what competing businesses are focusing their efforts on. So what you're really seeing is opportunities to get a leg up on the competition. As you can see above, rows 2 and 4 are extremely relevant to our real estate business and have low competition. These are two great trends to write about!

Two topics are great, and more is better. So now you want to find more related topics. Still using the Keyword Tool, use the option to search for new keywords using a phrase, website or category.

B	C	D	E
Keyword	Currency	Avg. Monthly Se	Competition
things to consider before moving in together	CAD	90	0.01
things to consider when moving out for the first tim	CAD	30	0.02
moving in together	CAD	5400	0.02
moving out	CAD	9900	0.06
moving out of home	CAD	1000	0.18
moving out for the first time	CAD	1600	0.03
first apartment	CAD	2900	0.08
first time renter	CAD	720	0.33
move in	CAD	9900	0.06
moving out of home for the first time	CAD	170	0.13
checklist for moving out	CAD	260	0.25
moving out list	CAD	320	0.14
moving in together checklist	CAD	320	0.13
things to do when moving	CAD	590	0.22
cost of moving out	CAD	210	0.16
moving out checklist	CAD	2900	0.22
moving out expenses	CAD	90	0.32
first time moving out	CAD	260	0.04
my first apartment	CAD	1300	0.16
first time apartment renter	CAD	260	0.41
list for moving out	CAD	90	0.24
first time apartment	CAD	210	0.21

You now have 380 keywords, for which you know the volume and competition.

As you build or grow your business, keep these tools handy. Use them when planning promotions, email campaigns, blog posts or any marketing content. They will give your business a serious edge.

The best way to explain how these tools work is through the below example of capitalizing on your off-season.

Chapter 1.7.1- Learning through an example

How to Capitalize on Your Company's Off-Season

Most companies and startups tend to pay less attention to the low season compared to the high season. Yet, in this day and age, if you are not present and active at all times, you are dead in the water.

Recognizing Your Off-Season

You probably have a good idea of your off-season, but remember that saying from earlier in the book - numbers don't lie. I would add to that, the more numbers you have, the clearer a picture of the truth you have. You may be basing your understanding of off-season on sales or traffic, for example, but what about search?

One of the best ways to predict when your off-season is, is to research search trends surrounding your product. To do so, look at both general industry trends and your own unique search trends through Google Analytics (we'll get deeper into Google Analytics shortly, and show you how to set up an account).

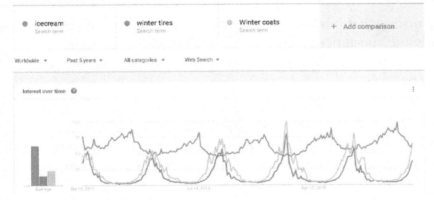

In the graph above, I selected three products (ice cream, winter tires, winter coats) that are all highly seasonal. By simply comparing the three charted lines, you can begin to see how seasonal changes can dramatically influence the demand for a product from one month to another.

These graphs, provided by Google Trends, will also allow you to understand user search behaviour from before, during, and after your high season. Equipped with this information, you can understand user-demand from an annual perspective and plan accordingly.

Now that you know your off-season, how can you handle it?

Use the time for buildup, preparation, and collecting leads for your high season.

If there's one important thing that I've learned with seasonal products and services, it's that you have to prepare for your off-season during your high season and prepare for your high season during your off-season.

During your high season, try to remember that, just as it is in the movie industry, the buildup is everything. So, as you are marketing for the high season, remember to collect as many leads, emails and followers as possible to cover your entire year.

Make sure that you appropriately market to these leads throughout the off-season in order to keep you and your product at the top of their minds. You don't want to be scrambling with branding and awareness campaigns right before a peak. Instead, you want to have laid the groundwork for strong brand recognition, so that you can take full advantage of the high season.

Never underestimate the off-season market. Don't stop your marketing in the downtime.

Never assume the off-season is a time to relax. During the off-season, the market is usually much less saturated, and the competition is less active. Use this to your advantage and push all forms of advertising throughout the off-season.

There is always a market that is not tapped into or is under-utilized. If you understand trends and consumer behaviour, you will be able to associate occasions (the specific time of year for your product) no matter how "off-season" they may be.

I recommend creating a marketing calendar up to a year ahead of time. I also recommend that you connect with one new person every single day in order to continuously expand your network. Come up with new content every week (either a blog, video, or podcast) and, on a larger scale, create a new campaign or event to invite people to every 45 days or so.

You may be thinking, "How on earth would you market winter coats during the off-season?" You could create content around proper cleaning and storage of winter garments (great for capitalizing on all those "spring cleaning" search terms), create funny videos of staff trying to "test" coats in the summer (maybe holding a staff meeting inside a walk in freezer), you could sponsor a charity event, or even partner with a business whose high season is summer in some unique way. Get creative and keep value and authenticity top of mind. Just remember that there can be value in humour, and a lot of humour to be found in juxtaposition.

Whether it be with an eBook, webinar, public speaking event, or anything else, the fact is: When you plan your calendar year accordingly, you are continuously coming up with new content and events to grow your network. And a larger network will help minimize your off-time purely by volume of users.

Trying, Measuring, Analyzing, and Updating

Never forget TMAU! Marketing has always been about trying, not about being perfect. It is always about testing out new approaches, new tricks, new creatives, new algorithms, etc. It's a constantly changing balancing act of try, measure, analyze and update.

What works now may not work in the next few weeks, months, or years. The only way to stay ahead of the game is by continuously trying new things.

As we mentioned earlier, your off-season is the perfect opportunity to test. Test website elements, landing pages, newsletter components... test everything, measure, analyze, update, then test again. Get all aspects of your business and marketing optimized and ready to take your next high season even higher.

Stay active, be present, be helpful and be supportive.

Above all, don't disappear. Your off-season is an excellent time to do behind the scenes TMAU work, but don't ignore your audience in the process. Keep your social media active. Keep your newsletter going. Keep adding new content, hosting events, giving promotions. Get creative, use the trend management tools, and find ways to be relevant, supportive, helpful, present and active.

Takeaway

Staying active, resourceful and present, whether it be on social media, blogs, forums, etc. is key to a successful off-season. Not only will regularly engaging with your user-base help build a great reputation and create loyalty, it will also differentiate you from your competition. No matter the time of year, always make time for your network, and the effort will pay off.

And remember, use more than one tool to get your data. Don't rely on only one source.

Chapter 1.8 - Are you taking full advantage of Data & Analytics?

Questions to ask yourself and business

Almost every business today has a web presence, and almost all of them have some form of data and analytics setup to measure the activity and/or effectiveness of that presence.

But, are you getting the FULL picture?

In my time working with entrepreneurs and small businesses, all the way up to Fortune 500s, I have come across far too many businesses that don't take full advantage of analytics. Often, they aren't even fully aware of what analytics can do.

The result? Missed opportunity after missed opportunity, competitors getting ahead, wasted resources and frustrated leaders wondering what piece of the ever-growing digital puzzle they're missing.

The most frustrating part is that getting fully up to speed on data and analytics is not a roadblock at all. It's surprisingly easy to overcome and doesn't require a technical background.

When you and/or your team master data and analytics, you are able to:

- Identify where visitors are coming from
- Which channels are sending the highest-converting visitors
- Where to invest more resources to increase quality traffic
- Where to cut resources
- Missed localization opportunities
- Partnership or advertising opportunities with high potential

See what visitors are doing once they arrive on your web property

- Map your various customer acquisition funnels

- See where people drop off so you can plug the leak

- Identify the pages with the highest conversion rates

- Identify important "under the radar" pages (for example, you may have an extremely low-converting page, but discover that it consistently sends high-converting visitors to your highest converting page)

Test practically every element of your pages and properties

- Which landing page converts best? What button colour gets clicked more? Do videos or images convert better? Best font? Best link text? Best menu style? Test. All. Of. It.

Identify hidden opportunities during your off-season

- Holiday or gift-giving cycles you may be missing out on

- Opportunities to strengthen page rank in preparation for stronger high seasons

- Branding opportunities to stay top-of-mind year-round

Build a data-driven content strategy

- Identify growing trends to be first on the bandwagon

- Discover high-converting but low competition keywords that are easier to rank for

- Use trend management to build a content calendar based on real numbers

- Identify and target new demographics and niches

Identify your top-performing content

- Shine a spotlight on it by incorporating links into your advertising campaigns, newsletters, blog posts, etc.

- Create more like it!

And this is just the tip of the data and analytics iceberg. There are many reasons why businesses don't invest in their analytics expertise. They think they aren't big enough for it, they don't realize how far technology has come, they think mastering it takes too much time or resources...

The truth is, every business can benefit from mastering data and analytics. It doesn't take a lot of time or resources to get started, and the size of your business doesn't matter. If you're already successful, analytics will help keep you in the top spot. If you're growing or just starting out, analytics gives you a considerable edge to succeed.

Sounds too good to be true? Here's the catch: you have to be prepared to put the work in. Once you've mastered the tools, reports, insights and how to act on all of it, you need to be ready to stick with it. Analytics is not one-and-done. It has to be a regular, ongoing part of your strategy to stay on top of an ever-changing market.

But, if you're willing to put that work in, the payoff is more than worth it. So, are you ready to take FULL advantage of analytics?

Digital Marketing

The ecosystem we are tracking & analyzing

Chapter 2.1 - Intro to digital channels

Digital Marketing Channels

Digital marketing is more than the Yellow Pages and search; it is a mix of different digital channels that you can use to promote and drive value to your business.

Digital marketing channels:

- SEO (Search Engine Optimization): The process of aligning the various elements of your site (tags, content, data, information, links, etc.) with the best practices of search engines, so that you can rank as high as possible in search engine results.

- SEM (Search Engine Marketing): The process of implementing search and display campaigns on advertising platforms such as Google Ads and Bing Ads, with the aim of creating relevant traffic and awareness for your brand and website.

- Social Media Marketing: The process of marketing your brand and website on social channels to create awareness, loyalty, retention, traffic and conversions.

- Most common social channels: Facebook, Twitter, LinkedIn, Instagram, etc.

- Email Marketing: The process of collecting email subscribers, then creating and sending email campaigns intended to grow brand awareness and sell more products and services, or otherwise convert subscribers such as encouraging event sign-ups, content downloads, etc.

- Common email marketing platforms: Mailchimp, Constant Contact, GetResponse, SendinBlue (this is a highly saturated market, and there are many to choose from)

- Content Marketing: The process of creating and sharing videos, articles, images and other forms of digital content.

- Local Marketing: The process of marketing your product or service to specific geographical locations or neighbourhoods.

- Landing Page Marketing: The process of creating highly targeted landing pages and directing traffic to said pages based on a set of predetermined criteria. The main goal of these pages is to get visitors to stay longer on your site and convert (buy, signup, etc.)
- Landing page marketing is also known as CRO or Conversion Rate Optimization.

We just covered the main types of digital marketing, but there are many more, with new techniques and tools evolving regularly.

For the sake of brevity, and in the interest of giving you the most 'bang for your buck', the marketing types listed above cover the bulk of what digital marketing is today.

It is important to know that these channels of digital marketing work best together. Alone, they will not yield great results. Combined, they become incredibly powerful.

For example, many people look at SEO as some kind of magic bullet. They'll say to me, "Tarek, I want to work on my site SEO. I want it to rank number 1, organically."

My answer is always as follows:

1. There are no guarantees in SEO so I can't promise you anything. What I can promise is to leave no stone unturned; no digital channel untapped.

2. SEO and search ranking optimization don't work on their own. Let's talk about your business and see how your other channels are working, or not working.

3. Let's talk about how your business can benefit the most from many different channels, instead of just one.

In short, don't expect to put all your eggs in one basket.

Which brings me back to analytics, what we will learn in this book is to track how all the different marketing channels will impact the performance of a web property across a specific period.

Takeaway

Digital marketing is a consistent, logical strategy. It's not, "Let's try this now and that later." For digital marketing to drive results, it must be holistic and consistent.

What role do data and web analytics play in digital marketing?

Analytics is the glue that holds all these channels together. It is what will help you gauge where you should invest your money, time and effort.

Throughout this book, you will learn how to capitalize on Google Analytics when it comes to each and every one of these channels.

Exercise

Create a diagram like the one in this chapter. Highlight the channels you are currently tapping into and which ones you need to start working on.

This will help you get a clear 360° view of what can be improved, what opportunities are being missed, and where you're doing well (remember that marketing is as much about celebrating the wins as it is about learning from setbacks).

Draw your business diagram here:

Chapter 2.2 - Things You Need to Know About Digital Marketing

Things you need to know

As entrepreneurs and business owners, we're always looking to take our businesses to the next level. Inevitably, digital marketing will come up as an avenue to evaluate. Despite being an avenue teeming with potential and opportunity, many entrepreneurs hesitate. **As a marketer, these are the reasons I hear over and over again:**

"It's just not the right time."

"My product isn't where I want it to be yet, so it's too early."

"I don't think it's the best ROI for me."

"I don't have the budget for digital right now."

"I just don't feel that digital is the way to go."

"My product does not need digital marketing."

My advice is this: If you haven't started yet, stop finding reasons not to and invest in digital marketing now.

Digital marketing is like vitamins for your business -- essential to growth. To compete and grow your presence, you need your vitamins.

Here are four things you need to understand about the importance of running digital marketing in parallel with product and service development:

1. Digital marketing doesn't have to cost an arm and a leg

One of the biggest benefits of digital marketing is flexibility. That flexibility extends to cost as well.

Successful digital marketing starts by creating authentic, unique and relevant content, which can be as simple and inexpensive as putting pen to paper (or fingers to keyboard).

Start with the question, "What keeps my target client up at night?" From there, start writing blog posts that address the questions and concerns they might have.

These kinds of posts boost search performance. As people search for answers to their questions, your website will show up. Depending on the blogging platform you use, these posts are also free, or very low cost.

Once you have your awesome content, ensure it's listed, categorized and optimized properly.

What does this mean? Use relevant tags for each post. For example, if you're selling pet products, use "pet products" as a tag. If the post is specifically about dog beds, use "pet products," "dog beds" and maybe "dog sleep solutions." Get it? Your blogging platform probably has a simple field for tags that you have to fill in.

Optimize your post by ensuring the title, headlines and content are aligned and reinforce the keywords you think people will most likely use in their searches. Consider a title like, "Top 5 Dog Beds for Canine Insomnia". You score "dog beds" and "canine insomnia" as keywords.

2. Digital marketing is as much about the buildup as it is about the kickoff

Building up to a product launch is as important as the launch itself.

Most successful marketers know how to introduce the right teasers, trailers and previews at the right time to get the hype up for a product or service release.

Take the movie industry, for example. Before a movie hits the theatre, you'll see at least one teaser, a few trailers and plenty of content spread across a certain time period. The build-up is sometimes even more intense than the movie!

How does this translate to entrepreneurs in other industries? You're probably not going to create Hollywood-esque trailers. Instead, cultivate a certain following on social media by sharing teasers about your upcoming product. Build traction using images and video on multiple channels. Use the power of social media to create excitement around your brand or concept and how it will change people's lives for the better.

Use teasers like, "The ultimate solution to conquering bathroom tile mould is just three days away!" Make it exciting. Make it intriguing. Throw some humour in if you can. Don't give it all away. Just get people interested.

3. Every product or service, no matter how good, needs digital marketing

The stats are staggering. According to recent statistics by Hootsuite & Internet World Stats, there are now more than 4 billion internet users worldwide. It's a playing field that can't be ignored. Seeing as most people are on the web and we're spending more and more time surfing on our phones than ever before, it simply makes no sense to overlook digital marketing.

No matter your ideal target, statistically speaking it's highly likely they are on the web, meaning opportunities exist to target them directly and effectively. Connect with them with the right content, at the right time, with the right message and you will reach a much bigger audience with much less investment than with almost any other marketing outlet. How do you know the right content and time? We'll be getting to that further along in this book.

4. You don't have to hire ten different agencies to run your digital marketing

You can start doing all of the above on your own.

When you're ready to invest a bit more, hire just one agency that will work with you to integrate SEO and content marketing. Many entrepreneurs hire two different agencies, but a good agency will do both.

When you marry your search strategy with your content strategy, it will yield a higher ROI for your business and, logistically, it's much easier to work with just one agency.

Takeaway

All entrepreneurs and small business owners should venture into digital marketing and should not wait for the 'ideal moment.' Nothing is ever perfect. It's about making the best of where you are now and moving forward.

The 'ideal moment' is now. It's always now. If you don't start now, someone else in your space will.

Exercise

Write down your business goals for this year.

The most effective marketing of any kind, digital or otherwise, is aligned with the goals of the business. When you are clear on your business goals, you can read this book with them in mind, and are open to the possibilities and opportunities that exist for you. This will help you understand how data and analytics will help you reach your goals.

Chapter 2.3 - Way of Thinking

The right marketing mindset

Before marketing became all about numbers, data, optimizations, trends and improvements... it was something else. It was a way of thinking.

So, before we jump into the data, let's explore the successful way of thinking when it comes to marketing.

Chapter 2.3.1. Think Value and Authenticity

Chapter 2.3.2. Think Education

Chapter 2.3.3 Think Mobile

Chapter 2.3.4 Think Speed

Chapter 2.3.5 Don't always think budget

Chapter 2.3.6 Think Intentions

Chapter 2.3.7 Think Local in your messaging

Chapter 2.3.8 Think first impressions

Chapter 2.3.9 Think Engagement

Chapter 2.3.10 Think building

Chapter 2.3.11 Think Customized

Chapter 2.3.1

Think Value and Authenticity

The most successful marketing brings value and authenticity. Successful analytics is about deriving the insight and intelligence to know how best to bring value and show authenticity.

In a world where everyone is trying to speak louder than everyone else, it is your values and your authentic brand that will speak loudest for you.

As you create campaigns, think about the emotions or motivations of your target audience. It's not unlike car ads. Sexy, sleek cars with beautiful, scantily clad women highlight a certain motivation beyond smart design or fuel-efficiency. Rugged 4x4's with young, fit millennials sell adventure, not advanced safety features. And minivans smartly loaded with camping or sporting equipment, complete with four smiling kids piling out sell family values. Identify the values of your audience, then build honest, authentic content that reflects the values you're bringing forward.

Providing value builds a relationship of mutual respect with your audience and a sense of camaraderie; a sense of "we understand and we're in this with you.".

Of course, profit is important. You're running a business after all. But making money cannot be the starting point of your marketing. The money may be your goal, but it isn't your audience's. When profit takes second place to delivering value, you connect with your audience more authentically, and profit will follow.

It is through giving that we become better as humans, and it is through delivering value that we become better as businesses.

72 | The Secret to Capitalizing on Analytics | **Tarek Riman**

Think Education

Teach something. Use the educational approach.

When a consumer has questions, they want to be helped, not sold to. And they are acutely aware of the difference.

They want to be educated, not pushed. Advised, not harassed. They will instinctively ignore an onslaught of advertising but engage with content that brings them value.

"But wait, I need to sell. That's how I keep the lights on!"

Of course, but remember that you're far more likely to make a sale if you give the customer what they want. And they are far more likely to talk to other people about it. Give them a good experience!

Be the face in the crowd that is educating and delivering real value. Provide tips, news and ideas relevant to your brand, product and target market.

What are your client's pain points? What are they stressing about? Create content that addresses these issues.

When you are seen as a source of knowledge, you are seen as an expert. When they feel that pain, they will also feel that you understand it and can help with it.

And all that great, educational content? Search engines love it too. By putting education first, you're putting that all-important value first, and that pays off for your business in numerous ways.

Think Mobile

The thing about mobile devices like smartphones and tablets is that they're... well... mobile. That's why most mobile search results are location-based.

Search for restaurant recommendations while you're at the office, for example, and you'll get results for restaurants in the immediate area. And when someone is looking for a good lunch spot while on the go, they're not going to go home to check their computer. They're going to whip out their phone.

That's why a responsive, easy to navigate and mobile-friendly site is an absolute must.

As a bonus, Google factors mobile-friendliness into their search rankings, so a mobile-friendly site can also improve your overall search rankings.

Not sure if your site is mobile friendly? Thankfully, there's a tool for that. Isn't the future great? Check if your site is mobile friendly here: **https://www.google.com/webmasters/tools/mobile-friendly**.

Chapter 2.3.4

Think Speed

Fact: Site speed and performance are becoming more and more important.
There are many reasons for that, but the most important are:

1. Making visitors wait even 4-10 seconds for a page to load will likely lead
    to a lost conversion.

2. All search engines consider site speed as a ranking signal.

3. No one wants to wait.

4. Our attention span is getting shorter.

5. We want everything now.

We're in an age of same-day delivery. We binge watch instead of waiting for
new episodes. We get our news when we want it instead of waiting for the next
broadcast. Some industries - like the food industry and the slow food movement
- are benefiting from a 'back to the old days' nostalgia. The internet will not be
one of them. If you want to compete, you have to be fast.

Don't Always Think Budget

A low budget is not an issue. Inaction is an issue. The most important thing is to start somewhere and measure results. Even a small investment will give you something to analyze and optimize, so that you can continue to improve results and drive more business. All you need is that first seed, and you can grow from there.

For local businesses to thrive, digital marketing is a must. Searching online is now the number one method people use to find the products, services and businesses they're looking for. You need to make sure they're finding you, and they're getting the best possible experience when they do.

Think Intention

Concentrate on intent, not just keywords.

As we move more and more towards voice search, mobile-first indexing, and machine learning algorithms, search, and SEO are becoming more and more... intentional.

At least in the sense that you must focus on the intentions of your market.

If the content you generate and share is going to successfully build strong SEO, it cannot be based solely on keywords. The intent of your audience must also be taken into account.

What do I mean by this?

The intention, in search, is about the meaning behind a search query and not simply the words used.

Let's say you are looking for a gym and type "gym" into Google. Go ahead. Give it a try.

Notice that Google doesn't give the definition of the word "gym". It doesn't give you the history of gyms, or even an alphabetical list of gyms.

No. Google anticipates your intention. It assumes you are looking for a gym in your neighbourhood. The first results you see will be the Google local listings for gyms near you, then a list of search results for gyms in your area and gym directories, typically listed based on an algorithm of user reviews, link popularity and many other factors.

Google's mission is, "To organize the world's information and make it universally accessible and useful."

For me, the most important part of Google's mission statement is the last two words: accessible and useful.

We are constantly moving to more relevant and smarter search results - results that are more and more accessible and useful. Relevancy, accessibility and usefulness depend heavily on understanding the intent of the audience, then planning your content and other marketing strategies around that intent.

As you look at the data within Google Analytics, Google Trends, or any data tool you use, remember that we have to think beyond the simple terms and clicks, and concentrate on what the users have in mind.

Chapter 2.3.7

Think Local in Your Messaging

Your messaging - the words, phrases and sentences you use on your site - has a big impact on your search results. Be sure to work your location into your messaging.

For example, if you are a Montreal-based photographer specializing in headshots, use phrases like "Montreal headshots," "Montreal headshot photographer" and "headshot photography Montreal." More generic phrases, like "headshot photographer," are too broad, difficult to rank for and don't capitalize on your location.

Think local in your messaging and you'll not only get much more relevant results, you'll also save time and money by not trying to rank for those broad, highly competitive terms.

Think First Impressions

For most businesses, brick and mortar storefronts are no longer a customer's first impression. People today go online to find virtually everything. Your website is now your first impression. And just as in real life, first impressions are everything on the internet.

Be ready for your customer's arrival. Just as you would keep a physical store looking its best, make sure your website is up to date, giving off the right impression and highlighting your most important information. That may be your mission statement, a call to action, instructions for how to contact you, a login form - whatever is most important for your customers to see first and foremost.

Think Engagement

Although "SEO" stands for Search Engine Optimization, the optimization you do is truly more for humans than search engines. After all, people are your customers. Not the engines.

To rank well, think about the human experience rather than the search engines. **Focus on human engagement**, relevancy to searchers, what will be most attractive to the people, rather than stuffing in keywords just to appeal to search engines.

Search engines do respond to a well-structured site with solid keywords and linking strategies. However, they also give weight to how visitors interact with your site - how often they click, how long they spend on your site, the number of pages they visit, etc. They also consider the types of sites linking to yours, and you are far more likely to have reputable blogs, businesses, e-magazines and even social media users linking to your content if it is engaging and delivers value. Those technical elements and other strategies targeting the search engines alone quickly lose their value in the "eyes" of search engines if real humans aren't showing interest.

Create for people and the search engines will follow.

Think Build Up

Many consumers look into new products or services before they are even released. Based on a Google study, moviegoers typically start looking into new movies a month before their release date.

The same is often true for product releases. Many consumers love a good product buildup. They read reviews, speculative blogs, watch videos and interviews, sign up for email updates, enter contests, and sometimes even pre-order so they can be among the very first to get the latest new thing. In your digital marketing efforts, this is a huge opportunity to build hype, brand awareness and engagement.

Probably the most well-known company to do this for products is Apple. Historically, they've done this really well and you can certainly look to them for ideas and inspiration. Just don't use Apple as your benchmark. They're a huge company with a massive following, and very few companies can match them. Instead, keep your focus on your target market. Where are they? What are they reading or watching? What are they searching for? What gets them fired up? Use that to create an engaging pre-release campaign that delivers value.

Capitalize on your pre-release period and you can carry that hype through into post-release. You don't need to be huge. You do need to be engaging.

Chapter 2.3.11

Think customized

Understand That There is No One-Size-Fits-All Approach

What you want to achieve and when you want to achieve it will differ from other businesses in your market. Your messaging will be different. Your creative will be different. Your corporate culture, quarterly objectives, and staff resources will all be different.

What works for one business won't necessarily be the right fit for your business. Approach all your marketing, including SEO and search marketing, in a way that makes sense for your business - its values, culture, objectives, mission and resources.

For example, building organic SEO establishes long term visibility, typically with higher conversions. But, it takes commitment and time before you see results. SEM (search engine marketing), on the other hand, delivers results only for your period of investment, but the results are more immediate.

What do you want to achieve? What are your resources? When do you want or need to see results? Understand this first before making any investment of time or resources.

Takeaway

Give before taking.

Intentions before keywords.

First impressions matter.

Exercise

Create a checklist like the one below to see where your thinking is aligned when it comes to your business and where it could be improved.

Ask yourself, "Is my business mindset aligned with a successful digital marketing mindset?"

MINDSET	MY BUSINESS MINDSET
THINK VALUE	
THINK EDUCATION	
THINK MOBILE	
THINK SPEED	
DON'T ALWAYS THINK BUDGET	
THINK INTENTION	
THINK LOCAL IN YOUR MESSAGING	
THINK FIRST IMPRESSION	
THINK ENGAGEMENT	
THINK BUILD UP	
THINK TAILORED APPROACH	

Chapter 3

Introduction to Google Analytics

Chapter 3.0 - Getting started with Google Analytics

Google Analytics

Up until now, I've been talking about why analytics matters, what it can do for you, why it's critical for business success, etc. Now it's time to get critical. What exactly is Google Analytics, and how do you get all that amazing data out of it?

Let's dive in.

To start, here are 3 acronyms to remember:

- **GA** = Google Analytics
- **SEO** = Search Engine Optimization
- **SEM/Paid Search** = Search Engine Marketing

Before I go any further, I'll include a side note for anyone who's reading this book to learn how to stalk or otherwise mine personal data: Google Analytics doesn't track personal information. What it gathers is known as non-PII data, which stands for non personally identifiable information. So, when I say that GA can tell you where your visitors live, what that means is that it can give you the breakdown of geographical information. For example, it can tell you that in July, 17% of your website traffic originated from the New York City area. It cannot tell you the names, addresses or any other potentially identifiable information about your visitors.

So, what is Google Analytics? It is a free website analytics service created by Google, following the acquisition of a company called Urchin in November 2005. It gives insight into how users find and use your website, as well as non-PII demographic information.

As of this writing, GA is the most used web analytics tool in the world. With GA, you can track ROI for your online marketing and gather intel to effectively boost ROI of future campaigns. The building blocks of GA reports are *dimensions* and *metrics*. Dimensions are the attributes of your data and metrics are the quantitative measurements for those dimensions. The main reason that Google Analytics is so popular is because it is a state-of-the-art tool. It is also, as of this writing, absolutely free, and when it comes to functionality, it can track almost anything that is connected to the internet, from eCommerce platforms, to mobile apps, to POS systems and beyond. It is also incredibly user-friendly and compatible with multiple other Google tools.

What You Need to Know Before Using Google Analytics

Like nearly everything else in life, GA requires you to have a Google Gmail account (which is also free). So make sure that you have that before you start.

Once you've got your Gmail account and have created your GA account, note that GA will only be able to track pages that have the GA tracking code embedded in them. If you want to track your whole website, every single page will need to have the code embedded. This is very easy to do, and there are many tutorials to be found online. If you have a website administrator, it's something they should be able to do within minutes. It should also be set up so that anytime a new page is created (a new blog post or landing page, for example), the GA code is automatically embedded in that new page. This, too, is very simple to do, and we'll get to the how-to shortly.

Who Needs Google Analytics

The last chapters walked you through just some of the awesomeness of analytics, but the number one reason to have GA on your website is that it analyzes the customer journey for you. Regardless of what you do online, even if your site is not an e-commerce site, GA allows you to track and understand your customer's behaviour. You put your website up with a purpose. Is it living up to that purpose? GA is how you get that picture, and how you identify opportunities to be better. The data you collect from GA will help you study your online presence and efforts so you can cater to your customers and take your business to the next level.

Here are just a few of the things it helps you accomplish:

- Understand where your customers are, geographically, and what devices they're using.

- Track which emails are bringing customers in, and which are not.

- Know what specific search terms bring in the most traffic for your niche.

- Compare traffic stats with competitors.

- Get reports on pages with high bounce rates.

- Know which pages have the highest conversion rates.

- Gauge which social platforms are bringing you the most attention.

- See your greatest sources of visitors and which sources send the highest quality of visitors (i.e. the ones most likely to convert).

Takeaway

We all need Google Analytics if we are to run, optimize or grow a business through online channels.

Chapter 3.1 - Success in GA Requires 3 Steps

Like all tools, GA is only as effective as the person wielding it. Take the time to get to know the tool and how best to use it within your business. These are 3 key steps you need to invest in to ensure success with GA:

1. **Setting up Google Analytics in the right way**

   - Creating a Google Analytics account

   - Customizing the account

   - Understanding the structure

   - Understanding how you can create views and properties for your account

   - Understanding how to distribute privileges

   - Understanding how to activate features

   - Understanding GDPR, privacy and Google Analytics

2. **Translating your data into insights**

   - Understanding metrics and dimensions

   - Understanding data hygiene

   - Knowing where to find relevant data

   - Understanding what this data means for your business

   - Understanding what is working and not working

   - Getting the most out of the data

3. **Acting on your insights**

   - Applying learnings to your business

   - Knowing how to react to data

   - Optimizing for better results

Lessons from GA Consulting

When I work with companies, I always work on getting to know the client first, understanding their business and their goals.

After that, I aim to create a Google Analytics account setup that is fully aligned with their goals.

To go the extra mile, I also help them with reporting, insights and dashboarding.

So, the process goes like this:

- Understanding who you are and what you want to achieve;
- Customizing your account to gather and compile data that's relevant to who you are and what you want to achieve;
- Creating reports and dashboards that give you easy-to-interpret visuals of what your data means.

But here's the crazy part: even though the client is the person in this equation who best knows the business, they always want me to be there to act on their insights, data and reports.

What this taught me is that data is more than just marrying our minds with numbers. In fact, it's not a marriage at all. It's more of a master and machine relationship. YOU are the master. You need to make the machine work for you.

Every time I sit down with a client's team to go over their data, we always end up with more than just the sum total. We always end up with genius ideas and actionable next steps. The data becomes an impetus to launch creative new ways to market and cater to customers.

The ability and drive to interpret and act on data is there, but for whatever reason, many people need to be led to the water, so to speak. Don't ever play the passive or reactive role to data. Be involved at every level. Data will not act alone. It needs you in the driver's seat. Get yourself in that mindset.

To bridge this gap between gathering the data and acting on it, I divide analytics consulting into setting up, researching and recommendations. For this, I like to use the metaphor of producing a Broadway play.

Setup. Read. Act. Here's how it goes:

Setup (Properly)

- Get to know the structure of your GA account.
- Learn how to create a Google Analytics account.

- Learn an alternative way of adding GA through a tool called Google Tag Manager.

Read / Understand / Analyze

- GA uses some terms you may be unfamiliar with. Learn the most important metrics and dimensions so that you are able to read the data on GA reports.
- Navigate the platform.
- Read and analyze GA reports.
- Understand the purpose of each report.

Act / Perform

- Act on the knowledge and insight they provide.
- Act on the data and analytics, by creating business and marketing decisions.

Takeaway

Having data without interpretation is like trying to perform in a play without a script.

Don't ever play the passive or reactive role to data. Be involved at every level. Know the tool, learn how to wield it, then do it.

Chapter 3.2 - Google Analytics Site Structure

How to Properly Setup Google Analytics

Google Analytics Structure

GA is divided into three levels.

The account level: This is where you label your group of properties. Every account can have up to 50 properties.

The property level: This is where you manage all your web properties. A web-property could be an app, a website, a POS, etc. Any property that is solely yours could be here. For example, you own your mobile app, so it can be tracked as a property. You don't own your Facebook page - that's the property of Facebook - so it can't be tracked as a property. Each property can have up to 25 views.

The view level: This is where you select the different ways you can view your property. One unfiltered view for every property in your account is automatically created. You can set up multiple views on a single property.

Let's use an example to better understand this structure:

I run a business called The Camino Within. Let's imagine it has a blog, speaking site, book site and a mobile app. These are all separate properties, meaning the blog, for example, is not embedded within the main website, but has its own URL.

The account name would be:

- The Camino Within

The property names would be:

- The Camino Within site - thecaminowithin.com
- The Camino Within blog - blog.thecaminowithin.com
- The Camino Within travel app - IOS & Android apps
- The Camino Within speaking site - speaking.thecaminowithin.com

A good example of the views could be as follows:

- All data view
- Canadian visits
- International visits
- External traffic only
- Backup view

With views, you apply filters so that you only see the data you want within that view. This makes it really easy to quickly extract your most relevant and frequently needed information. Just note that when you're in a particular view, you won't be able to retrieve any information that you've set to be filtered out. You'll need to remove that filter or choose another view. Also, be sure to label your views very clearly.

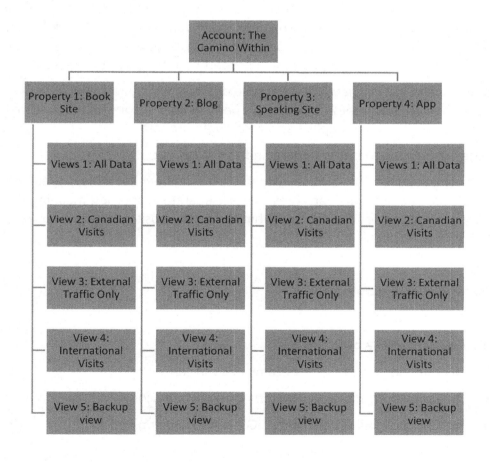

As you will learn further along in this book, this structure is important for permissions, account management, integration and accessibility. For this reason, take care that your GA structure makes sense for you, your business and your business objectives.

Takeaway

Google Analytics account structure is an important factor in collecting and compiling the data most relevant to your business goals, in a way that makes sense for you. When set up properly, it will help considerably in the long-term planning, preparation and performance of your business online.

Exercise

Create the Google Analytics account structure for your business and make sure that it makes marketing and business sense. Don't worry about what will actually be shown in the views or how you'll filter data just yet. We'll get to that later on. For now, just determine the type of views you want.

We will need this structure for the coming chapters.

Chapter 3.3 - The GA Setup
Tips for Designing your structure.

Tips for Designing your structure:

- Keep in mind that GA is there to serve your marketing and business strategy.
  As much as the setup is important, it is more important to check it daily. Most successful marketers and business people check their analytics almost daily. It usually guides their decisions to be more data-driven. As you design your structure, think about how you will use it daily.

- Don't forget the purpose of data and GA. The main reason to use GA is to make sure visitors are doing what you want them to do on your site or web property. This could be a contact form submission, sign up to a newsletter, buy a product, request a quote, etc. When setting up GA remember your KPIs and goals for the site.

- Remember that a big strength of GA is the ability to integrate with all the other Google tools. Keep in mind that you will likely be connecting your GA account with Google Ads, Google Search Console, Google Tag Manager, Google AdSense, etc.

- Another strength of GA is the ability to customize reports to your needs. As you go through the process of setting up GA, keep in mind how you want to view the data. Better yet, always bear in mind who will benefit from what report. When we approach the end of this book, where you'll learn how to customize data, bring these thoughts to life through the right dashboards.

- Through GA, you can compare data across different months, traffic sources and other dimensions. As you analyze different reports, remember to make data more relevant through comparing.

- Remember that GA can do (much of) the work for you. You are better off creating intelligent alerts to notify you of a rise or drop in traffic or any other significant change with your site data, rather than relying on manual daily checks.

Google Analytics Permissions

As mentioned earlier, Google Analytics structure is important when it comes to giving permissions and delegating rights to teams and individuals. For example, you may want to permit some people to view reports, but not make changes within the Google Analytics platform, whereas you may want to grant someone else permission to edit dashboards and create filters. The structure is a key part of that.

You can delegate four types of permissions in GA. Permissions can be granted at any level of the GA structure (Account, Property and View). Permission types include:

Manage Users (Permission): This allows someone to remove and add user access to the account.

This is a dangerous right to handoff, especially given the fact that if you grant this level of permission, you might be kicked off the account yourself. Ideally, only one person should be able to add and remove users. This way, you have better control over who has access, and what level of access they have, to your incredibly valuable data.

Edit (Permission): This allows someone to edit accounts, properties and views, filter data, and create goals. The only thing they can't do is manage users. This permission level is ideal for Analytics experts.

Collaborate (Permission): This allows someone to edit shared dashboards or add annotations. This permission level is ideal for marketers, social media managers, and campaign managers.

Read & Analyze (Permission): This is a read-only level. It allows someone to read and view reports, but they cannot make any changes. This permission level is ideal for CEOs, managers, etc.

Note:

It is important to note that while you can grant permission at either the account, property or view level, that permission is hierarchical. That means, if you grant someone permission at the property level, they will automatically have access at the view level as well. Grant it at the account level, and they automatically have it at the property and view levels.

Let's start by setting up GA properly on your site

Google Analytics Account Creation. (Without GTM*)

GTM stands for Google Tag Manager. It offers an alternative method of setting up GA. We'll review that in the next section.

Let's use the example of The Marketer Within. This is the title of a book I'm currently writing, and I eventually intend for it to have three web properties: a site for the book itself, another for its blog, and another for a related marketing academy.

Before creating the account, we need to plot its structure.

So, we have three properties:

- themarketerwithin.com (Book site)

- blog.themarketerwithin.com (Blog)

- TMWAcademy.com (The Marketer Within Academy)

For each one of these properties, we would like to have two views to get us started.

- Backup view (Once you filter something out in GA, you cannot get it back, so it's a good idea to create a backup view with no filters at all. That way, if you need something down the road, it's there in the backup view.)

- Filtered view (Here we'll filter out any bots, internal traffic, etc.)

This is how the structure would look:

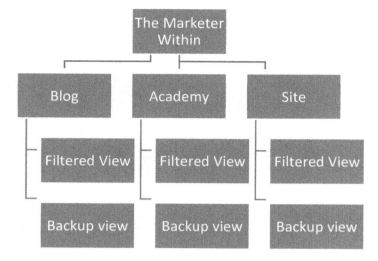

Once we've plotted the structure, we create the account.

1.   **Go to https://analytics.google.com**

Click register, and you should be led to step 2. Remember that you will need a Gmail account to register, so do that first, if you have not already.

2.   **Fill in the information as shown below.**

We want everything to be as clear as possible, so we will name the account "The Marketer Within". We'll continue this example using the book site property, and will name that property "The Marketer Within Book". You could also opt for something like "TMW Book Site" or 'Book - The Marketer Within." Just make sure it's clear and ideally a consistent naming structure for all properties.

Once we name it, we'll add the URL of the property, the category and the time zone.

The time zone is important as it will determine how your reporting appears.

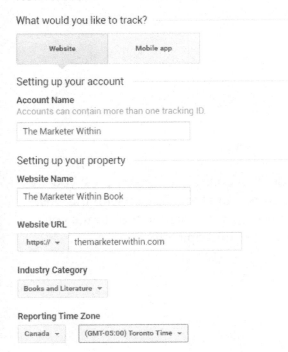

New Account

What would you like to track?

| Website | Mobile app |

Setting up your account

Account Name
Accounts can contain more than one tracking ID.

The Marketer Within

Setting up your property

Website Name

The Marketer Within Book

Website URL

https:// ▾ | themarketerwithin.com

Industry Category

Books and Literature ▾

Reporting Time Zone

Canada ▾ | (GMT-05:00) Toronto Time ▾

3. **You will be asked after to agree on Google terms and conditions.**

☑ I accept the Measurement Controller-Controller Data Protection Terms for the data that I share with Google.

| I Accept | I Do Not Accept |

As much as we tend to ignore reading the terms and conditions and just click agree, I urge you to read this one. There are a lot of rules around user privacy and you owe it to the visitors of your site to mention that you are tracking their behaviour. Mention this in your privacy policy and a popup upon arrival at your page.

I am not a lawyer, but with the recent updates regarding the GDPR (General Data Protection Regulation) and Privacy Update, you are required to read the terms and agreements and upgrade your site accordingly. Don't worry that this will disadvantage your business in any way. All businesses that operate a web-property are expected to comply with these regulations, and it is simply good business ethics to be honest about your tracking.

4.   You will then be provided with your tracking code.

Copy this code and paste it to the headers section of your site code. If you are unfamiliar with editing site code, get a professional to help you with this. Just remember that it is a very simple and quick task. If someone tries to tell you otherwise, I strongly recommend getting a second opinion.

<HEAD>

<GA code goes here>

</HEAD>

5.   Time to test!

Never assume something's working. Always test! The best way to do so is to go to the GA real-time report.

If you go to the left-hand column in GA, you will see a clock icon, which represents real-time reporting.

Real-time gives you insight into what is happening on your site right now.

So, if you go back to your site and refresh the browser, you should be able to start seeing the visits coming in. Here's what it might look like:

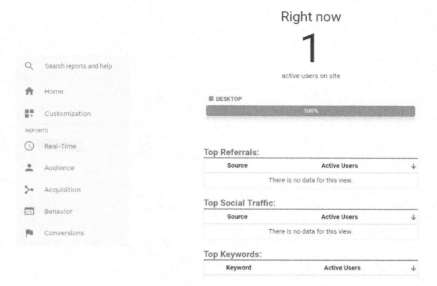

If you see an active user, that's you! Congratulations. You now have Google Analytics properly embedded in your site.

Of course, if your site is live, you may see more than one active user. Those would be all your current site visitors. However, if you see zero, that indicates a problem. Go back and verify that you've added the code in the correct place, and that you have not accidentally modified the code in any way.

Exercise:

Using the structure plan, you created in the previous chapter, create your Google Analytics account, with your property/properties and views.

Add the tracking code to your site, and run a test.

Chapter 3.4 - Google Tag Manager

Adding your site to Google Analytics through GTM

GTM stands for Google Tag Manager.

As the name implies, this is a tool for managing the tags on your site.

What are web tags? They are pieces of code used to collect information from a web property. One type of tag is a web tag, which can also be called a tracking pixel or analytics tag. One example of a web tag is the little snippet of the GA code that we looked at in the previous section.

Google Tag Manager is also known as a tag container. Like a physical container, it holds multiple things. In this case, multiple tags, from multiple channels.

Google Tag Manager helps us, as marketers and business owners rely less on developers, as we don't have to enlist the help of developers to add tags to the site. This will avoid major delays since it doesn't have to go into development pipelines and processes.

All we have to do is add the Google Tag Manager snippet to our site once; then we are all set.

It is extremely important to understand that Google Tag Manager doesn't replace Google Analytics. It complements it.

GTM Implementation

In this exercise, we will go through the creation of GTM for a site and then connect GA to it.

Again, we'll use the example of The Marketer Within, with the following URL: https://themarketerwithin.com/

To get started, head to Google Tag Manager:

https://tagmanager.google.com/

If you have a Gmail account, you will be prompted to sign in.

If you don't have a Gmail account, get one, then sign in. When you sign in, you will be prompted to create a GTM account.

Q   CREATE ACCOUNT

When you click "Create Account", you will be prompted with an "Add a New Account" window. Fill in the account name and country, and hit continue.

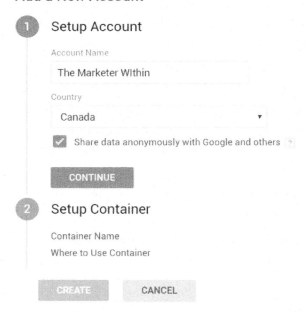

Add a New Account

1   Setup Account

Account Name

The Marketer Within

Country

Canada   ▼

☑ Share data anonymously with Google and others ?

CONTINUE

2   Setup Container

Container Name
Where to Use Container

CREATE   CANCEL

Then enter your container name.

Typically, you use the URL of your site without the https:// part. In this example, that would be "themarketerwithin.com".

Next, select "Web" under "Where to Use Container."

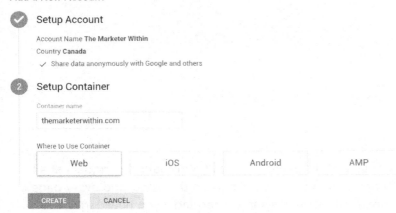

You will then be prompted to add the Google Tag Manager code to your site.

Note that the code must be added in two different places within your site code. Paste the first box of code as high in the <HEAD> section of the site code as possible. Place the second box of code immediately after the <BODY> tag in your site code.

After you press "OK", you will arrive at the Google Tag Manager dashboard.

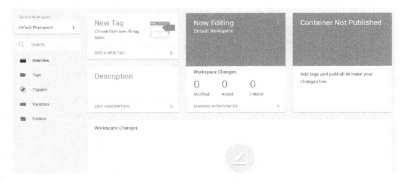

For the sake of this example, we will create a tag that automatically triggers at all the pages on the site. That means, you only have to do this once, and every page within your site will automatically have the tag embedded, even new pages you create down the road.

Click on "Tags" and "Create New" to create a new tag

Now name your tag. A great name is "GA Tracking Tag." Remember, our aim is clarity.

Next, click "Tag Configuration." (Choose a tag type to begin setup).

As you can see, a window appears prompting you to choose your tag. If you scroll down, you'll see that you can add different types of tags to GTM. They don't have to only be Google-related tags.

Click on "Google Analytics – Universal Analytics"

Under the "Google Analytics Settings" menu, choose "Select New Variable."

This will prompt you to add GA settings, which is where you copy the account number that was generated for you back in Google Analytics. Paste that number under "Tracking ID."

This tracking ID can be found above the tracking code that was given to you by Google when you created your GA account. See the image below:

After you paste that code, name your variable - I named mine GA - then click "Save".

After saving, you'll be sent back to the tag page. You'll see that your tag is all set, but you still have to choose where you want it to trigger.

Creating a Trigger

In GTM, "Trigger" means on what occasion you want a certain tag to fire.

When you click on "Triggering" (choosing a trigger to make this tag fire), you will be brought to a window like this:

✕ Choose a trigger

Name	Type
◉ All Pages	Page View

If you want your whole website to be tracked (which is what we want in this example, and what is typically the case for most websites), you will select "All Pages". You'll then be sent back to the previous page with an overview of the confirmation of both the trigger and the tag.

Press save and your tag, variable and trigger will be ready.

Publish

"Publish" means to put it live - into action. Now that you have your tag, variable and trigger, you are ready to publish.

Once you're back at the main dashboard, click "Submit."

You will be led to add a description, which I do recommend adding as it will help you keep track of changes in the future, or across your team. Then click "Publish."

You now officially have GTM added to your site, with GA up and running through an embedded tag. Congrats!

You still need to test that it is working, which you'll do the same way as explained in the previous chapter, via real-time reporting.

Important Note:

If you already have GA on your site and decide to switch to GTM, make sure to first remove the previous GA code from the site.

If you don't, you will be tracking duplicate content and skewing your data.

Takeaway

Google Analytics and Google Tag Manager complement each other.

Additionally, using GTM can eliminate the need for developers or site admin to get involved every time a new page needs GA code, which can significantly speed up the process, so that you can start measuring ASAP.

Exercise

Create a Google Tag Manager account.

Add Google Tag Manager tag to your site.

Add Google Analytics to Google Tag Manager. (Just remember to remove any pre-existing GA code first.)

Run a test on your site.

Chapter 3.5 - Google Analytics Important Terms
Reading / Understanding

GA Important Terms

The next step is to understand GA better so that we can transform it into relevant insight for our business.

This is the part of Google Analytics that I call the practice. To practice, we get familiar with the important terms: the critical metrics and dimensions that you should learn before you are able to read the actual data on GA reports.

This practice will help you get familiar and comfortable with the GA reports that we will cover in performance later on.

Our goal is to translate data into actionable insights. To do that, you need to understand what you're looking at.

- **Users** = Visitors. These are the total number of people arriving on your site or page during a specified time period.

- **New Users** = New visitors. These are your site or page visitors who have never visited your site before.

- **Sessions** = Visits. Each visit is a new session. If someone arrives on your site, checks out a few pages, then closes their browser window or otherwise leaves your site, that is one session. If they open your site again, that's the beginning of a new session.

- **Returning Users** = Users – New users. These are people who have visited your site before and are now coming back.

- **Pages/Visit (Session)** = The average number of pages viewed by people after hitting a particular landing page.

- **Average Visit (Session) Duration** = The average total time spent on the website during a session.

- **Bounce Rate** = The percentage of visitors that viewed only this page, then left your site without doing anything else.

Dimension	Metrics					
	Acquisition			Behavior		
Default Channel Grouping	Users ↓	New Users	Sessions	Bounce Rate	Pages / Session	Avg. Session Duration
	3,842 % of Total: 100.00% (3,842)	3,773 % of Total: 100.03% (3,771)	4,455 % of Total: 100.00% (4,455)	82.69% Avg for View: 82.69% (0.00%)	1.33 Avg for View: 1.33 (0.00%)	00:01:05 Avg for View: 00:01:05 (0.00%)
1. Organic Search	2,588 (66.72%)	2,558 (67.80%)	2,855 (64.09%)	83.75%	1.29	00:01:01
2. Social	626 (16.14%)	576 (15.27%)	780 (17.51%)	83.72%	1.36	00:00:59
3. Direct	447 (11.52%)	442 (11.71%)	504 (11.31%)	81.75%	1.34	00:00:54
4. Referral	206 (5.31%)	188 (4.98%)	303 (6.80%)	72.61%	1.59	00:02:17
5. Email	10 (0.26%)	8 (0.21%)	10 (0.22%)	60.00%	1.90	00:01:07

The above graphic shows what a typical GA report looks like. The terms we just covered will help you understand it.

Metrics in this table are there to describe dimensions.

A dimension can be a traffic source (like search, social media, paid ads, newsletters, etc), or a language (the language of your visitors - note that Google doesn't actually know someone's spoken language, but it can know the language setting on their browser), or any other attribute of your site performance.

Looking at the metrics of a dimension gives you valuable insight into your property performance. For example, it can tell you which traffic sources give you the most engaged, high converting visitors, and where you might need to improve (or even cease efforts). You may know that an overall campaign performed well, but drilling down dimensions in GA can tell you which elements performed best. You may find you're getting significant traffic in a particular language, but visitors are bouncing because your site isn't optimized for multiple languages. This insight can be incredibly valuable and help you concentrate your resources where they will have the most impact.

How is GA divided?

- Audience: Who is visiting your site
- Acquisition: How visitors arrive on your website
- Behaviour: How visitors interact with your website
- Conversions: How visitors complete (or do not complete) conversions on your site

Because every business is unique with unique needs and objectives, Google provides a huge range of data collection and reporting options. Once you're more comfortable with GA, you'll be able to more easily sift through the options and identify those most valuable to you.

As GA is so extensive, it would take thousands of pages and many hours of your time to go over everything. For the sake of this book, we'll keep it to the most essential reports that will help you in your campaigns and in kicking off your marketing and analytics knowledge. These will give you a good foundation to start and grow from.

Exercise:

Google knows the importance of practice. They also know you don't necessarily want to practice on "the real thing". That's why they've created a demo account specifically for people new to GA to get familiar with the tool. So let's practice!

Go to the Google Analytics Demo Account:

https://analytics.google.com/analytics/web/demoAccount

Navigate through the metrics and get familiar. Remember the terms from the beginning of this chapter.

Chapter 3.6 - Google Analytics Admin

An overview of Google Analytics administrative section

As discussed earlier in the book, Google Analytics has three levels.

Account, Properties and views

 These levels are visible when you visit the admin section of your Google Analytics account. See below:

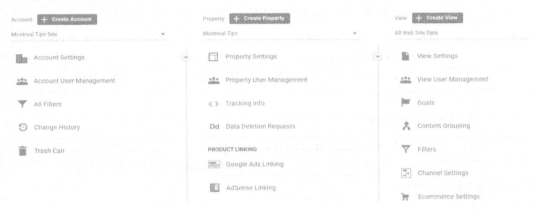

These levels are divided into three columns, and in each column there are settings associated with each level.

In this chapter, we will go through the most commonly used settings of each of these levels.

Let's start with the account level. As we go through the different settings, I advise you to go to your Google Analytics account and navigate to your admin section, which can be reached by clicking on the blue gear at the bottom left corner of the screen.

Account-level settings:

The Account admin section includes:

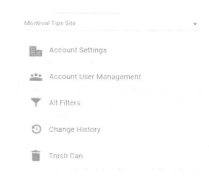

- Account settings

    o In this section you get your account ID wish is unique to your account and will be used as part of the property ID when it comes to tracking code.

    o You can also change your account name. This happens when you do a rebranding to your business.

    o You can choose your country of business.

    o You can update your data sharing settings; it is a way to control how you share your Analytics account data with other Google products and services. I personally keep it to default.

    o There are also amendments to data processing here that you have to abide by, especially if you are in certain countries. E.g. GDPR, which requires you to make changes on your web properties.

- Account user management

    o It is where you can add users to your Google Analytics account. Any user at this level will have access to all the other levels.

- All filters

    o Is a place where you can add filters at the account level. I tend not to add any filter at this level unless I find something essential. However, I highly recommend adding filters for the view level.

- Change history

    o It is a changelog of all the administrative changes done on the site.

    This includes the date the change is made, who is it changed by, and what was the change. See example below:

Date ↑	Changed By	Change
Feb 21, 2020, 11:26:45 PM	tarekriman@...	Property "Montreal Tips" default URL changed from "http://www.montrealtips.com" to "https://www.montrealtips.com"
Dec 25, 2019, 5:08:40 PM	tarekriman@...	Goal "Stayed more than 2 min" created on property "Montreal Tips" on view "All Web Site Data"

- Trash Can

- This is where you can find anything that has been deleted at any level of your account. You have the option of restoring it if need be.

Property Level Settings

The property admin section includes:

- Property settings:
    - Tracking ID, which includes the Account ID we have seen in the account level setting married with property ID.

UA-43685658-*1 – the bold part is Account ID, the Italics part is the property ID.*

The UA stands for Universal Analytics

    - You can change the property name.
    - You can change the default URL
    - You can change the default view.
    - You can update your industry and category.

The question is when do we change these, and the truth is not often. The few times that I have seen these changes were after a site migration to a new URL.

It is important to use the same property when you get a new URL, as you need to keep the old historical metrics for the sake of better reporting.

There are some additional settings to attend to under the property settings:

    - Allow manual tagging (UTM values) to override auto-tagging (GCLID values) for Google Ads and Search Ads 360 integration

I recommend enabling these settings as manual UTM tags are usually set for one-off campaigns. We will be discussing this in detail later in the book, where we talk about Social media and Google Analytics.

- Property user management
    - It is where you can add users to your Google Analytics property. Any user at this level will have access at all the view level
- Tracking Info (Tracking Code) This is where you pick up the tracking code that you can use in the site header of the GTM Tag, that you will be placing on your web property.

Product Linking (Subsection of Property Settings)

This is known as the Google Analytics Product Linking section, where you can link other Google products to Google Analytics for ultimate reporting.

These products include AdSense, Google Ads, Google Search Console, and a few others.

In most of my properties, I tend to link these 3.

- Audiences Definition

In this section you can create specific audiences based on their behaviours. We will go more in-depth on this topic in chapter 3.8 on creating audiences for remarketing.

In a nutshell, using this option will allow us to remarket to specific audiences on whether they visited specific pages or took a particular action or navigated a specific product.

View Level Settings

- View settings:
    - o You can see the view ID
    - o Rename the view after it has been created.
    - o Delete the view
    - o Copy the view to create a similar one
    - o Update the view website URL.
    - o Update territory and time zone.
    - o Choose a currency.
    - o You can filter out bot traffic which means that you will be excluding all hits from known bots and spiders. Which I highly recommend.
    - o You can activate Site Search Tracking, which will allow you to see what people are searching for on your site.

- View user management
    - o It is where you can add users to your Google Analytics property. For me, this is the area that I give access to when it comes to working with other agencies, or even internally. I limit access to the view level; that way I can maintain the security of the account.

- Goals
    - o This is where you need to set up your goals across the account. We have covered that as part of the conversion reporting of analytics.

- Filters

- Here is where you set view specific filters. And based on my experience, this should be the only place that you apply filters in.

- As we discussed earlier in the book, it is important to have a back view with raw data, a filtered view and a master view.

- Segments

  - This is where you can add specific segments to the account, yet it is better to do so in the reports itself, where we are going to cover this in detail.

  - Yet this is a good place to see the list of all segments and clean up any redundant filters across the accounts.

- Annotations

  - Annotations in Google Analytics are ways of leaving remarks on changes made to that might impact the results we see.

  - Common annotations examples:

    - Starting an SEM campaign

    - Starting Social winter campaign

    - New SEO optimization rollout

    - New site rollout.

  - These annotations are important so we as marketers can attribute specific results to specific action done.

Analytics Reports

Digital marketing Analytics Reports.

"Installing analytics and customizing it properly without checking it regularly is like having a Ferrari in the garage and never using it." – Tarek Riman

Analytics is about acting.

Chapter 4.0. The Audience Report

Chapter 4.1. The behaviour Report

Chapter 4.2. The Acquisition Report

Chapter 4.3. The Conversion Report

Chapter 4.4 Every Business Reports

Chapter 4.5 Segments

Chapter 4.6 Remarketing and Audiences

Chapter 4.0 - The Audience Report

Google Analytics Audience Report Overview

The audience report reflects what type of audience you are getting to your site.

Under the audience report category here is what you can find:

Audience Overview Report

As the name suggests, this is a broad overview of your audience, meaning the people visiting your site or property. It provides the following metrics:

- Users
- New Users
- Sessions
- Number of Sessions per User
- Pageviews
- Pages / Session
- Avg. Session Duration
- Bounce Rate

For me, this is definitely the one to watch. It's one of the most important reports on the platform, as it helps you know if there is something wrong on your page within seconds. If your bounce rate is up, visitors are down, traffic has stopped...these are things everyone needs to know right away, regardless of your unique business objectives.

This is also my go-to channel when I need to start creating a report for a client, as it gives a quick overview of the overall status of the traffic on the site.

Audience Demographics Report

This is a great report when it comes to building profiles of your visitors to better create targeted, relevant content, and to identify potential marketing or business development opportunities with greater relevance to your audience. Remember that GA does not collect identifiable information about people, but it can give you a general breakdown of your visitors' ages and genders.

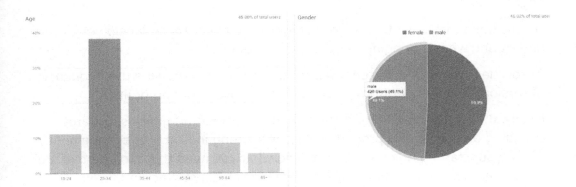

This report is especially helpful for paid search campaigns. If you intend to run Google Ads, Bing Ads or other paid search campaigns, details from here will help a lot in narrowing down your ideal markets and yielding higher ROIs.

Audience Interest Report

Google tracks and collects so much data. This includes people's interests, which can be gleaned through their online navigation and purchasing activities. Again, this is not identifiable information. You won't know that Frank down the street is in the market for a new lawnmower. Instead, you'll get averages and breakdowns. In the graphic below, you can see the Affinity Category, In-Market Segment and Other Categories reports.

This report is particularly helpful when it comes to creating display or paid social campaigns, where you are given the option of adding interest and target marketing affinities.

Audience Geographic Report

This report provides both location and language-based reports, allowing you to not only understand what cities/countries your clients are visiting from, but also what languages they are using.

This is especially useful when you are creating content, as it will help you choose the most popular languages, and to target content to specific cities or geographical locations.

This is also useful when you are launching a campaign, as it helps you determine which cities will bring the highest engagement or ROI. Rather than spreading your resources thin, you can focus your investment where it will have the most impact.

Audience Behaviour Report

This report highlights new visitors, returning visitors, frequency & recency, and engagement.

For me, the most important metric is new vs returning. This will help you understand what is bringing people back to your site.

As for the Frequency & Recency report, this is useful in showing the frequency of sessions that you get from particular visitors over a period of time.

Finally, the Engagement Report shows you the amount of time visitors are spending on your site or property, which is a strong indicator of engagement. This is your starting point for determining what you need to do to improve the visitor experience on your site, drive more high-quality traffic, and turn unsuccessful visits into more successful ones.

Audience Technology Report

This report shows the browsers, operating systems, screen resolutions and screen colours of all the devices used in visiting your web property.

This report is especially helpful in measuring site performances across different devices. This matters if you have visitors coming to you via large-screen desktop computers, smaller laptops, tablets and/or smartphones because your content and site elements can be displayed differently depending on the device displaying them.

This report can also come in handy if you are trying to pinpoint a problem in site compatibility.

If we take the browser report below, for example, we can see that some of the browsers do have higher bounce rates than others. This could be a sign that the site could be improved for better visitor engagement, or that there are elements not rendering properly on certain browsers.

Browser	Acquisition			Behavior		
	Users ↓	New Users	Sessions	Bounce Rate	Pages / Session	Avg. Session Duration
	10,744 % of Total: 100.00% (10,744)	**8,685** % of Total: 100.08% (8,678)	**13,063** % of Total: 100.00% (13,063)	**37.29%** Avg for View: 37.29% (0.00%)	**4.88** Avg for View: 4.88 (0.00%)	**00:03:06** Avg for View: 00:03:06 (0.00%)
1. Chrome	**8,107** (76.01%)	6,356 (73.18%)	10,102 (77.33%)	33.80%	5.21	00:03:25
2. Safari	**1,665** (15.61%)	1,495 (17.21%)	1,946 (14.90%)	46.66%	4.04	00:02:05
3. Firefox	**281** (2.63%)	254 (2.92%)	330 (2.53%)	44.55%	3.65	00:03:03
4. Edge	**151** (1.42%)	141 (1.62%)	174 (1.33%)	56.90%	2.83	00:01:59
5. Samsung Internet	**107** (1.00%)	98 (1.13%)	130 (1.00%)	47.69%	3.58	00:02:05
6. Safari (in-app)	**84** (0.79%)	83 (0.96%)	87 (0.67%)	75.86%	1.97	00:00:46
7. Android Webview	**83** (0.78%)	83 (0.96%)	89 (0.68%)	65.17%	2.65	00:00:44
8. Internet Explorer	**70** (0.66%)	66 (0.76%)	73 (0.56%)	49.32%	3.99	00:01:44
9. Opera	**51** (0.48%)	50 (0.58%)	55 (0.42%)	60.00%	2.76	00:01:23
10. UC Browser	**18** (0.17%)	18 (0.21%)	18 (0.14%)	66.67%	1.67	00:00:23

Audience Mobile Report

This report displays the performance of desktop vs. mobile vs. tablet.

Also, under the devices sub-section, you can see the type of mobile devices used to browse your web property.

This report is especially important if you are selling products or services through your site as it will reflect the behaviour of users across different devices and will detail the type of devices most commonly used, so that you can better optimize your web property for those devices.

This report also reflects which device categories bring in more traffic vs. ROI.

From a marketing standpoint, this will help you know where to better spend your money.

Audience Users Flow Report

This report displays the flow of users through the different pages of your web property. The best part about this report is that you can choose a dimension upon which to base the user flow. This comes in handy in many ways. For example, if you find that visitors coming from paid search campaigns have a higher than usual bounce rate, or lower than usual conversion rate, you can use this report to get an idea of how they are interacting with the site once they arrive, and potentially identify what is causing the problem. Often, when a campaign or effort doesn't yield positive results, we abandon it. But, if we can get a better understanding of why it didn't drive results, we can potentially adjust course and open a whole new avenue of leads or sales.

As in the example below, you can see that I chose source/medium as my dimension. This will allow me to see where users come from, what they are visiting and how.

Exercise:

Go back to the Google Analytics Demo Account.

https://analytics.google.com/analytics/web/demoAccount

Create a persona based on all the findings that we went over from the audience report. A persona is a general outline of a market demographic. It takes data and humanizes it, helping you better understand your audience and better target them in the future. Below are some sample personas to help you get an idea of the practice.

Sample personas:

Example 1: Andrew

A young professional living in San Francisco who is passionate about technology, media & entertainment.

Demo: Male, 25-34 years old

Geo: English US, lives in San Francisco, CA

Lifestyle: Value shopper, technophile, media & entertainment lover, business professional

Product-purchase interests

- Consumer electronics (mobile phones), business & productivity software, employment, business services (advertising & marketing)

Specific interests

- Arts & entertainment, internet & telecom, reference resources, online communities

New visitor

- Google/organic (16.93% conversion rate)
- Devices: **desktop (29.85%)** & mobile (12.93%)
- Browser: Chrome
- Visited pages: Men's apparel | Brands | Accessories | Shop by brand - YouTube

Goal Conversion rate of Source/Medium for 25-34 age bracket:

- Google/organic (16.93%)
- Direct/none (31.90%)
- mall.googleplex.com/referral (56.68%)

Example 2: Mya

A millennial living in India, interested in social media, technology and cyber security.

Geo: Lives in Karnataka, India

Demo: Aged 25-34

Lifestyle: She's enthusiastic about new technology, software products, entertainment and celebrity news

Additional Details:

She's a Facebook user and enjoys online shopping on her iPad.

Mya is a returning visitor. She clicked on a Facebook post and browsed YouTube's branded products, but didn't make a purchase (high bounce rate of 58.40%).

Mya loves Google's Nest® products. In 2017, she did a direct search on the Nest® Cam Outdoor Security Camera at an average price of $120 (low bounce rate of 28.04%).

In 2018, she returned on the site where she did a direct search on the Nest® Secure Alarm System Starter Pack at an average price of $349.00 (low bounce rate of 25.25%).

Mya is likely to convert on products relating to home security.

Example 3: Chris

A young Canadian who spends a lot of time on his smartphone, occasionally shopping for trendy clothes while on his laptop.

Geo: Lives in Toronto, Ontario, Canada.

Language: Speaks Canadian English.

Demo: Aged 18-24 years old.

Additional details:

- Shops mostly for warm men's gear and bags
- Likes trendy brands; looks for the latest best thing
- Saw Facebook ads and now visited the website to purchase (returning visitor)
- Uses mobile phone for online browsing

Example 4: Sam

A middle-aged California male who is interested in self-development and the "Silicon Valley" lifestyle.

Geo: Lives in Mountainview, CA

Language: Speaks English.

Demo: Aged 45-54

Device: Google Pixel 2XL

Additional details:

- Interested in Lifestyles & Hobbies for Business Professionals, as well as employment-related searches indicating that he may be in pursuit of further career opportunities, or in developing his career-related aptitudes.

- A returning visitor, this is Sam's second visit to the site. His first visit was from an ad on Facebook via his Apple iPad; the second was a direct search via his desktop PC.

- His probability of conversion rate is high, at 87.64%.

Example 5: Ana

A Euro baby boomer interested in connecting more on the web.

Geo: Lives in Berlin, Germany

Language: Speaks English, German.

Demo: Aged 55-64

Device: Her first search was on her Google Pixel 2, the second was on her desktop PC

Interest: Health and Fitness, Marketing and Advertising, joins online communities and enjoys social networking.

Additional details:

- A returning visitor, this is Ana's second visit to the site.

- First visit was from an affiliated search where she landed on the site browsing for accessories for housewares (high bounce rate 48.52%).

- Second visit was a referral link she clicked on from YouTube's Creator Academy Channel (high bounce rate 63.97%).

Source: Spice Girls Team from my class at Concordia University.

Chapter 4.1 - The Acquisition Report
Google Analytics Acquisition Report Overview

The acquisition report reflects how people are coming to your site.

As a marketer, entrepreneur and business owner, this is one of the main reports that I rely on for my site because it gives me the best picture of where new users are coming from and where I need to concentrate efforts to drive the best ROI possible.

Acquisition Overview Report

This report allows you to see the best sources of traffic to your site and how visitors from these specific sources are interacting with your site.

In other words, you get insight into what's working and what's relevant.

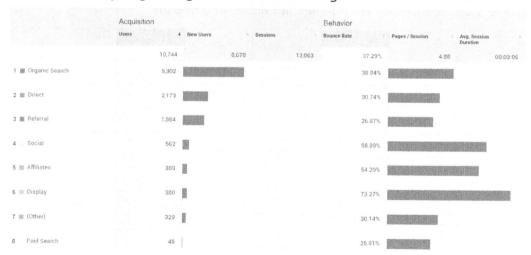

Acquisition All Traffic Report

This report allows you to see, in detail, how traffic from specific channels, sources and mediums are behaving on your site.

As you can see in the report below, we are shown both the behaviour and the acquisition metrics associated with specific sources and mediums.

Source / Medium	Acquisition			Behavior		
	Users ↓	New Users	Sessions	Bounce Rate	Pages / Session	Avg. Session Duration
	10,744 % of Total: 100.00% (10,744)	8,685 % of Total: 100.08% (8,678)	13,063 % of Total: 100.00% (13,063)	37.29% Avg for View: 37.29% (0.00%)	4.88 Avg for View: 4.88 (0.00%)	00:03:06 Avg for View: 00:03:06 (0.00%)
1. google / organic	5,145 (46.44%)	4,254 (48.98%)	5,976 (45.75%)	38.20%	4.84	00:02:56
2. (direct) / (none)	2,178 (19.66%)	1,809 (20.83%)	2,657 (20.34%)	30.71%	5.10	00:03:40
3. mall.googleplex.com / referral	1,125 (10.15%)	506 (5.83%)	1,483 (11.35%)	12.27%	7.96	00:04:51
4. analytics.google.com / referral	572 (5.16%)	393 (4.53%)	665 (5.09%)	54.89%	2.61	00:02:33
5. Partners / affiliate	389 (3.51%)	344 (3.96%)	441 (3.38%)	54.20%	3.22	00:02:05
6. dfa / cpm	380 (3.43%)	356 (4.10%)	419 (3.21%)	73.27%	2.10	00:00:58
7. creatoracademy.youtube.com / referral	349 (3.15%)	336 (3.87%)	356 (2.73%)	67.42%	2.24	00:00:46
8. (not set) / (not set)	329 (2.97%)	235 (2.71%)	355 (2.72%)	30.14%	5.42	00:02:52
9. baidu / organic	89 (0.80%)	88 (1.01%)	90 (0.69%)	84.44%	1.56	00:00:26
10. groups.google.com / referral	59 (0.53%)	32 (0.37%)	88 (0.67%)	28.41%	5.31	00:03:56

This is a goldmine for marketers as it can help identify the mediums that work and the mediums that don't. And, in case you haven't spotted the trend yet, a huge part of GA's value is in its ability to help us see clearly, and on a granular level, what's working and what isn't, so that we can respond accordingly and continually take our businesses and web properties to the next level.

Acquisition Referral Report

This report allows you to see, in detail, which websites are linking to yours and the amount of traffic that these sites are sending to yours.

Source	Acquisition			Behavior		
	Users ↓	New Users	Sessions	Bounce Rate	Pages / Session	Avg. Session Duration
	2,439 % of Total: 22.70% (10,744)	1,522 % of Total: 17.54% (8,678)	2,984 % of Total: 22.84% (13,063)	33.45% Avg for View: 37.29% (-10.31%)	5.42 Avg for View: 4.88 (11.14%)	00:03:28 Avg for View: 00:03:06 (11.77%)
1. mall.googleplex.com	1,125 (45.96%)	506 (33.25%)	1,483 (49.70%)	12.27%	7.96	00:04:51
2. analytics.google.com	572 (23.37%)	393 (25.82%)	665 (22.29%)	54.89%	2.61	00:02:33
3. creatoracademy.youtube.com	349 (14.26%)	336 (22.08%)	356 (11.93%)	67.42%	2.24	00:00:46
4. groups.google.com	59 (2.41%)	32 (2.10%)	88 (2.95%)	28.41%	5.31	00:03:56
5. m.facebook.com	57 (2.33%)	56 (3.68%)	59 (1.98%)	67.80%	2.17	00:00:39

This is especially important if you are working on your site's SEO and on link building as it can be a great reference of site SEO performance, as search engines do take into account the number and quality of external links leading to your site.

It can also help you identify potential partnership or advertising opportunities based on the quality of traffic external sites are sending your way.

Acquisition Google Ads Report

This report allows you to see, in detail, how your Google Ads paid campaigns are performing and how they are yielding results on your site.

Under the Google Ads report (previously Google AdWords Report), you can see the performance of the account, campaigns, sitelinks, final URL, display, video, shopping and keywords.

Highlighting all the critical attributes of a Google Ads campaign, this report opens the door to not only understanding what is bringing clicks, but also to understanding what keyword, account, ad or campaign is yielding higher engagement on the site.

To have proper access to this report, you have to link your GA account with your Google Ads account. This is not done by default.

To link them, navigate to the admin panel in GA and, under the property panel, select "Google Ads linking". A list of your AdWords accounts will show up. Check the one that you want to link, click continue and you're all set.

If you don't have an AdWords account and aren't sure if you want or need one, don't worry. We'll explore AdWords a little more later on to help you determine if it's right for your business.

Acquisition Search Console Report

This report provides you detailed information on the performance of queries, pages, devices and locations in Google organic/natural search results. Organic search is simply the unpaid search results that come up on Google or other search engines when someone enters a search term. They are differentiated from the paid results that are often displayed at the top or side of search engine results pages.

Similar to the Google Ads report, you have to set up this link, as it is not provided by default. The message below should appear when you attempt to access this report without the link:

This report requires Search Console integration to be enabled.

Set up Search Console data sharing

What is Search Console?
Search Console is a free product that provides data and analytics to help improve your site's performance in Google search.

Enabling Search Console data within Analytics
Once you connect a site you own in Search Console to your Analytics property, its data becomes visible in your Search Engine Optimization reports. You can visit the Property Settings page in Analytics account management to change which of your Search Console sites' data you wish to show, and control which views on your Web Property have access to view the data.

How to use Search Console data within Analytics
Search Console provides data about what users see in Google search results before they decide to click to your site (or some other site). You can use this data to identify opportunities and prioritize development effort to increase the number of visitors to your site. Examples:

- Identify landing pages on your site that have good clickthrough rates (CTR), but have poor average positions in search results. These could be pages that people want to see, but have trouble finding.
- Identify search queries (keywords) for which your site has good average positions, but poor click through rates. These are queries for which your pages get attention and improved content could lead to more visitors.

Click on "Set up Search Console data sharing" and you will be brought to the property setting page. Scroll down until you see "Search Console":

Search Console

Click "Adjust Search Console" and you will be redirected to a page where you can add the associated Google Search Console property.

Search Console Settings

Search Console site (?)
By linking your Analytics property to your Search Console account(s), Search Console data will be imported in Analytics and included in your Google Analytics reporting. Learn more
none & Add

Done

Click "Add" and you will see a full list of your Google Search Console properties.

○ https://montrealtips.com/	This site is not linked to any web property in your Google Analytics account.
○ http://www.montrealtips.com/	This site is not linked to any web property in your Google Analytics account.

Click the property that you want to integrate with analytics and click "Save". You will then see the following message:

Add association

You are about to save a new association. Any existing Search Console association for this web property will be removed.

OK   Cancel

Press "OK" and you're all set.

Note: If you don't have a Google Search Console account, we will cover that in Chapter 11 (Google Search Console Setup).

To verify that the connection was successful, go to admin panel > property > product linking, then click "All Products." You should see something similar to the following:

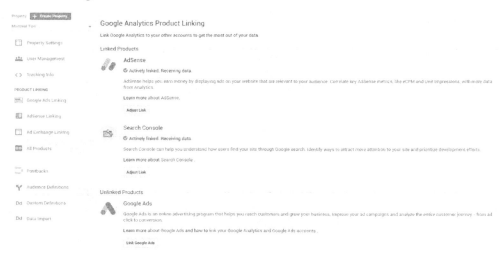

Now that you have access to the Google Search Console data, you can start seeing not only what keywords and pages are bringing the most organic traffic to your site, but also how engaged the visitors on these pages are and whether or not they are converting.

Acquisition Social Report

The social report allows you to identify your most successful social networks and campaigns in terms of bringing traffic and conversions to your web property.

The report highlights social network performance, your best performing landing pages, conversions driven from social channels, and the user flow for visitors arriving from these social channels.

Social Network	Sessions	% Sessions
1. YouTube	388	60.82%
2. Facebook	118	18.50%
3. Google Groups	80	12.54%
4. Quora	24	3.76%
5. reddit	17	2.66%
6. Pinterest	4	0.63%
7. wikiHow	4	0.63%
8. Twitter	2	0.31%
9. Google+	1	0.16%

It is important to note that GA qualifies YouTube, Facebook, Google Groups, Quora, Reddit, Pinterest, WikiHow, Twitter, Google+, LinkedIn, Blogger, Pocket and VK as examples of social networks.

When it comes to social networks, I find that landing pages tend to be big players, as we often link to specific pages in our efforts and campaigns rather than simply our homepage. As such, I find the greatest value in the social landing page aspect of this report, as it is one of the best ways to figure out which landing pages are best or worst when it comes to performance and engagement.

Acquisition Campaign Report

This is one of the most accurate and specific reports when it comes to traffic acquisition for your web property.

It is a centralized report highlighting campaigns from social, paid search, display and any tagged URL. You will also be able to see all URLs that you have UTM tagged.

What is a UTM tag? UTM stands for Urchin Tracking Module, but don't get caught up on the "Urchin" part. "Tracking Module" is what's relevant here. A UTM tag is a bit of code that you add to the end of a URL to track specific campaigns. If you were running a Facebook campaign, for example, you would add a UTM tag to all links used for that campaign, enabling you to track results. Without the tag, results from the campaign would be lumped in with all Facebook traffic and you would not be able to isolate them to accurately measure results.

Exercise:

Go to the Google Analytics Demo Account.

https://analytics.google.com/analytics/web/demoAccount

Complete the following exercises:

- Identify the traffic source with the highest level of engagement.
- Identify the source that is sending the most traffic to the site.
- Identify the top-performing keywords.
- Identify the top-performing social channel.

Chapter 4.2 - The Behaviour Report

Google Analytics Behaviour Report Overview

The behaviour report provides insight into how people are interacting with your web property.

Among the many insights you can glean from this report are:

- What is engaging visitors when they arrive on your site
- What pages they visit during a session
- How fast your pages load for them
- The visitor behavioural flow
- What content keeps users most engaged
- What visitors are unable to find and what are they looking for through your in-site search
- What specific events/actions your visitors are taking on the site

This can be one of the most important reports and is definitely one to concentrate on when your objective is to get people to stay on your site longer, or to funnel them to a specific action.

Information in this report gives you the insight to effectively improve the user experience, user flow, loading time, and the UX/UI attributes of your site or web property.

Behaviours Site Content Report

Simply put, this report provides you with the engagement metrics associated with each and every single page on your site. It provides insight into how people interact with your site, what holds their attention, how much time they're spending with your content, etc.

Behaviour Landing Page Report

A landing page is the first page a visitor sees when they land on your site. This won't always be your homepage as you will likely link to internal pages for different campaigns and marketing efforts, as well as have other businesses, blogs, media outlets, etc. link to various pages within your web property.

The landing page report is a content marketer's BFF. It instantly shows how well each of your web pages is performing, empowering you to identify the content that performs best, and which does not.

With this report, you can identify which pages on your site earn the most traffic, and how well each page converts visitors into leads or customers.

As you can see in the example below, this report reflects the most popular, engaging and converting landing pages on your web property.

This report is especially helpful when you are creating a paid campaign and want to get the most bang for your buck, as it will help you identify the best pages to link to.

Behaviour Exit Pages Report

This report is like your own personal snitch. It gives you insight into your property's bounce rate by telling you when visitors exit your site, and which pages visitors most commonly leave from.

This is really helpful, as a high exit rate is a red flag that a particular page is either not engaging enough, or that there may be some other issue with the page like a longer than usual load time, broken links or some other under-performing element that needs attention.

If you're working on improving your site's conversion rate, this is one of the reports you'll want to dig into, as it gives you insight into what does, and does not, convert.

Behaviour Site Speed Report

The Site Speed Overview gives insight into how your site is performing from a load-time perspective. As we covered earlier in the book, we are very much in an "on-demand" era, and a site or page must load instantly if it's going to keep visitors engaged.

Through GA, you are able to test your site speed over every single page of the site.

The example report here shows a site that is quite fast, which is ideal for eCommerce sites that are aiming to improve the overall site flow.

Under this report you can access the page timings report to get more page-specific insights. Additionally, GA will provide you with suggestions for improving the speed of each page under the speed suggestions section.

Behaviour Site Search - Queries Report

This report shows what is being searched for on your site. For this report, you will need to have Site Search integrated into your web property. Site Search is a Google product that adds a search widget to your website. This allows visitors to search for things within your site.

If you have Site Search capabilities built-in, Site Search metrics are the best way to see what people look for once they have arrived on your site.

Are people searching for something you don't have a lot of content on? Or maybe you do, but they're using different terms and not finding what you have?

This is an important report as it will help you understand what your site is missing, and identify opportunities to improve the visitor experience in order to boost engagement and conversions.

It is one of the best reports for working on your CRO (Conversion Rate Optimization).

Behaviour Site Search - Search Pages Report

In this report, you will get insight into what pages visitors are using Site Search from.

This insight can help you see what pages didn't meet visitor's needs or expectations, or what pages piqued their curiosity and got them hunting for more.

Using the insights from this report, you can make informed improvements to optimize the pages getting the most Site Search activity.

Behaviour Site Search Usage

This report breaks down the number of visits where Site Search was used vs. those where Site Search was not.

This is an important ratio and, while there is no golden ratio, when I see that more than 3% of my traffic is using Site Search, it's a sign that improvements are in order.

Takeaway

The Behaviour Report is your relevance report.

If visitors are happy or unhappy with what they encounter on a visit, the best way to know is through how they interact (or don't interact) with your site. Once you know, you can respond.

Exercise

Go to the Google Analytics Demo Account.

https://analytics.google.com/analytics/web/demoAccount

Complete the following exercises:

- Identify the pages with the highest bounce rates.
- Identify the page with the highest exit rate.
- Identify the most used keywords in Site Search throughout 2018.

Look at all the data you've collected. What improvements can you potentially make to the pages in the site to increase the time spent on-site?

Chapter 4.3 - The Conversion Report

Google Analytics Conversion Report Overview

A conversion in GA is when a visitor to your web property completes an action that you value in terms of business objectives.

There are 2 types of conversions in GA:

- A micro conversion - Usually a small conversion that will eventually lead to a macro conversion. What this conversion will be depends on the site, but it could be something like a newsletter signup or ebook download.

- A macro conversion - This is the conversion you deem most important on your site or web property. Someone making a purchase could definitely be a macro conversion, but it could also be something like filling out a contact form or registering for an event.

GA allows you to set goals for conversions. This is a very useful feature, but also, conversion reports only work if you have these goals set up.

There are 4 different types of goals that you can create in GA:

- Destination (i.e. visitors getting to a specific page)

- Time on site

- Pages per visit

- Event (an event can be watching a video, sharing content, commenting, adding a rating, adding something to a cart, etc.)

Creating a Goal

1st Goal Creation Example

Go to the Admin directory and choose "Goals" under the view column.

Click "New Goal".

Select "Custom", then "Continue".

I'll first enter a goal name. When creating your own goals, remember the importance of clarity and ensure the name is something you can easily identify later on when reading reports.

For this example, I will use "Engaged Visitors" as the goal name.

After the goal name, I'll set a duration and hit "Continue".

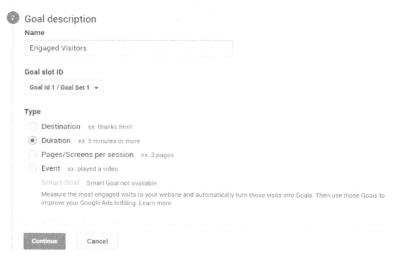

Why duration? In this case, I want to set a goal of keeping people on the site longer. That's how I'm defining engagement.

Under "Goal details" I will input a duration of greater than 1 minute and 30 seconds as the threshold for which I will count this visitor as an engaged one, and consider the event a successful conversion (i.e. goal met).

Next, I hit "Verify goal" to see if this goal is actually viable. GA determines viability by mining historical data. In this case, it tells me that based on trends from the past 7 days, this goal is likely to have a 7.24% conversion rate, meaning approximately 7.24% of all visitors will spend at least 1 minute, 30 seconds on the site.

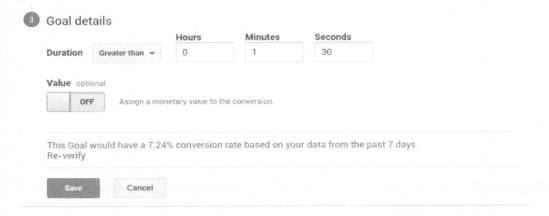

I'll then click "Save" and we're all set to track our goal conversions.

2nd Goal Creation Example

For this example, repeat the steps from the previous example up until "Goal description".

In this example, I'll create a goal for my book site.

When someone completes a purchase through the site, they are redirected to a "Thank You" page, so I'll use the URL of that page to indicate a successful conversion.

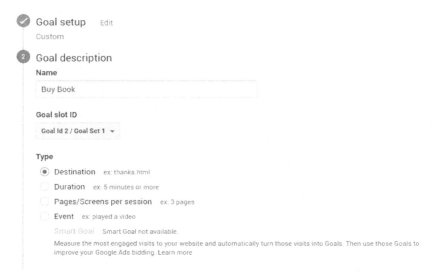

This time, I'll use "Destination" as my goal type and the URL of the Thank You page as my destination.

You'll see in the graphic below that you don't need to enter the full URL. You only have to enter the page extension. In this case, the full URL is http://thecaminowithin.com/thank-you, but I've only entered /thank-you.

I then add the value I want to associate with this goal. In this case, I will use a monetary value, that being the purchase price of the book.

I hit "Save" and my second goal is all set.

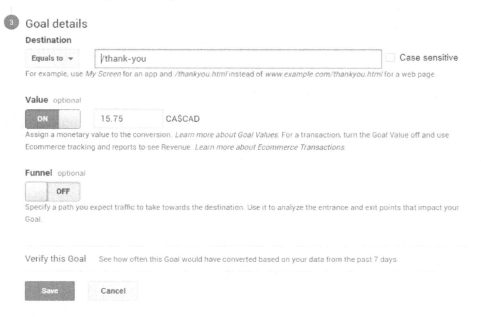

In this example, I've created just two goals, but I urge you to create more. Keep testing out different goals and customize them based on what makes the most sense for your business structure and objectives. Remember, what gets measured, gets managed. If you want to achieve something, measurement is your first step. This way, you'll know where you are and how you're progressing, and be able to quickly flag any roadblocks to that progress.

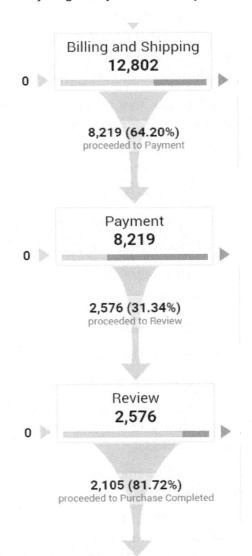

When you are all set, go back to the Conversion Report where you can begin to analyze the data. Just keep in mind that you'll need those goals to be running for a little while before you get any data to analyze.

Conversion Goal Overview Report

This report allows you to get a quick overview of which goals worked and which didn't.

It also shows the location, source or medium that led to the most conversions.

Conversion Goal URLs Report

This report shows from which URL the majority of goal completions occurred.

Conversion Reverse Goal Path Report

This report shows the most popular path to goal completion on your site or web property.

Conversion Funnel Visualization

This report shows the flow of visitors in, out and through the goal funnel, until they reach the final conversion.

Conversion Goal Flow Report

This report shows how traffic was driven from specific dimensions to specific pages, leading to the final conversions.

These reports are so important as they give you a good idea of what is converting most, who is converting most, where you are missing the target when it comes to site flow, how to improve ROI, and what you should be capitalizing on.

Conversion Attribution Model Report

This is yet another invaluable report, as it highlights the visitor journey across different sources and pages leading to your site or web property.

An attribution model is the rule, or set of rules, that determine how credit for conversions is assigned to various sources or touchpoints in conversion paths.

For example, let's say someone clicks on a paid display ad and buys my book through the book site. Great! Display ads are working! However, that was not that person's first encounter with my site. Their first encounter was through social channels. They didn't convert that time, but they did come back again through a Google search, checked out a few pages, then left again. The display ad visit was actually their third visit to my site.

So, which channel gets credit for the sale?

When we talk about "attribution", we're talking about the channels to which we attribute conversions - the ones that get the credit.

Within GA, there are different models we can use for attributing conversions. Here are the different models:

- Last Interaction

- Last Non-Direct Click

- Last Google Ads Click

- First Interaction

- Linear

- Time Decay

- Position Based

In my experience, the most valuable models are:

- Last Interaction: In the book example above, the last interaction would be the display ad. That's where we would attribute the successful conversion using this model.

- First Interaction: In the book example, that would be the social channel that drove the first visit.

- Linear: This gives credit to all involved channels equally. In the book example, that would mean the social channel, Google search and the display ad each get an equal percentage of the credit attributed to them.

Using these three attribution models, you start to build a picture of where your most valuable traffic originates, which sources are pushing the most conversions and insight into how your different channels work together to drive conversions. Attribution models matter because a traffic source or touchpoint may not be the originator of conversions or the final push, but it may still be playing a role in driving conversions. You need to be aware of it, so that it gets the attention it deserves.

You can also use this report to help you concentrate a different message for each part of the journey. Meaning, if you realize that paid search is doing great from a first interaction standpoint, then good. Continue investing in paid search as an awareness channel.

If you see that social networks are doing great on the last interaction model, then you might consider a remarketing campaign to capitalize further on this channel.

The main goal here is to see what is working and to be constantly tweaking, improving and testing for maximum conversions.

Takeaway

Conversions are the most important metrics in Google Analytics. They are what keep your business growing.

Setting up your conversions and goals properly will help you build a clearer picture of what is working, what isn't and what opportunities to capitalize on.

Exercise

Go to the Google Analytics Demo Account.

https://analytics.google.com/analytics/web/demoAccount

Complete the following exercises:

- Identify the highest converting goals.

- Identify the micro-conversions in place.

- Identify the macro-conversions.

- Identify the highest converting landing page.

- Identify the point in the conversion funnel where the most conversions are being lost.

Just by extracting these insights, you'll begin to develop a good feel for what matters most and potentially what you can do to drive more successful conversions.

Chapter 4.4 - Reporting with your business in mind

Reporting with your business in mind

Analytics (or GA) presents us with an interesting challenge where, once we set it up, we suddenly find ourselves with more data than one person can reasonably sort through. Now, GA also filters that data into handy reports and charts that make it easy for us to analyze and act on, but here again we're faced with the challenge of an abundance of report options to choose from. With only so much time on hand, where do we direct our focus for maximum impact?

Before diving in, you first want to remember the purpose of your website, which is to attract, engage, inform and ultimately drive business to you. We then want to remember the true power of GA, which is to show you exactly what's working, what isn't and where your best opportunities for optimization are.

With that in mind, here are the top five Google Analytics reports that every business should keep on their radar:

1. Acquisition Report

This report shows you the top channels sending you visitors (a new visitor = a new acquisition) as well as the conversion rates for each of those channels so that you can quickly identify your top performing channels and those where you can investigate and optimize.

This is the report that will tell you if your investments in channels like social media or Google Ads are paying off, if your SEO efforts are yielding results, etc. It will also show you what areas are not driving results, so that if you haven't done any work there, you can start, and if you have been working at it, you know to take a deep dive and reassess those investments.

2. All Traffic Report

This is where you can really start to drill down on your traffic sources. Whereas the Acquisition Report groups sources into channels such as Social Media, Organic Search and Affiliates, All Traffic lists the individual sources, such as Facebook, a linked article, a newsletter, etc. So, while Social Media, for example, may be your overall best traffic source, the All Traffic Report may reveal that only one social network is sending all that great traffic while the others are lagging behind and sources like linked articles or partner sites are actually performing quite well.

One of the best parts is that the information comes in in real-time. You don't have to wait weeks to see results and decide what action to take. You can see, right away, if a new effort is working (which could also signal you if there are technical issues like a broken link) and see the trend over time.

3. Home Report

This is the default landing page when you first sign into GA, and it's like your executive report. It gives you a super quick overview of your site stats so you can see, at a glance, how your site is performing and how it has changed. Right away, you'll see how many users and visits you've had over the last seven days, your conversion rate, revenue (if you have that set up) and the change from the previous week.

You'll also see your top acquisition channels, your busiest and slowest times of day and a few more key stats. These numbers are very high level, so it's a good one to check daily for a quick update. If you do check daily, it can also show you right away where any major changes have happened so that you can drill down and investigate.

4. Site Speed Report

Site speed matters for two very important reasons. First, it has a big impact on user experience. We live in a time when people expect instant results. If a site is taking too long to load, it's frustrating for people to navigate and try to engage with the content. What happens? They leave.

Which brings us to the second reason site speed matters: search engine optimization. Search engines like Google and Bing pay attention to user experience as a factor in the value of a website. If your site is taking too long to load, they know users aren't going to like that, and your rankings may start to drop, or at least not improve.

A slow loading site can increase your bounce rate, lower your conversion rate and overall negatively impact your site's performance. A sudden drop in site speed is also a red flag that something is wrong on the technical side that needs investigating. Watch this report! You don't want to find out too late that your site has become unusable.

5. Site Search Report

Site search is your insite search - the little search box people can use to search directly within your site. If you don't have site search and you have more than just a few pages, I highly recommend setting it up.

Why is this report so important? Good content is one of the most powerful elements of a website. It engages visitors, gives them a reason to come to you and stay with you, helps convert visitors to customers and can significantly improve your search rankings. How do you create good content? By knowing what people want! That's where site search comes in.

When people use your site search, they are literally telling you what they want; what they're looking for; what matters to them. Using the site search report, you'll see exactly what people are looking for when they come to your site, which tells you exactly what kind of content you need to create to better serve your visitors and the search engines.

There is so much power in Google Analytics and so many opportunities to uncover and capitalize on. It's easy to get lost in the data and miss the forest for the trees. But, if you start with these five reports, you get that big picture to start from, which points you in the right direction to start drilling down with intention. This is how you excavate that actionable data that truly helps drive your business forward.

Chapter 4.5 - Segment
How to use segments to get better analytics

Segments are one of the most underutilized tools in Google Analytics, and it is for that reason that in most of the classes I teach, I concentrate on segments as one of the cornerstones of measuring persona behaviours consistently.

Segments are not only great tools to measure performance in Google Analytics, in fact they can be exported into other tools to help simplify customization.

For example, Google Data Studio.

Segments are subsets of Analytics data. Meaning your analytics data represents 100% of your visitors to the site; a subcategory could be males from age 35-45, which represents 17% of your visitors, and that in turn is a subset of your total visitors.

In analytics, you have a wide variety of ways in which you can set up your segment.

As a business, you need to create segments as they will let you dive in and analyze personas, behaviours and campaigns, which will help you optimize specific aspects of your business accordingly.

When you set up a segment, you can apply it across any report in google analytics, and it will remain there until you remove it.

Also, you can activate four segments at the same time, which will enable you to compare them side by side.

Let's take the following business scenario: we are a retailer, and we want to see how our 43 target markets have performed in the previous month.

Persona 1: Daniel

Lives in USA, 35-45, Interested in sports & travel, Male

Persona 2: Melissa

Lives in Canada, 25-44, Interested in shopping, Female

Persona 3: Mike

Lives in the UK, 25-35, interested in technology, Male

So how do we create a segment?

If we are to create segment we can do so from any report, as long as you are inside Google Analytics , you are able to navigate to the top part of the page and click on the "+ Add Segment" sign next to the "All User" Tab, see below:

As you click on "Add segment" you will be prompted to fill in details about your segment/persona.

You can easily get lost with the wide choices that you have, but you have to remember that if a segment is not scalable enough, then it is not worth measuring, so avoid checking or filling in a lot of the options. Make sure that you stick to your persona that you are aiming to research. For example for the persona below you can see how we choose the age group, gender, interest and location.

When it comes to segments here are the list of options that you have:

-   Demographics where you Segment your users by demographic information. Includes:

    o   Age

- Gender
- Language
- Affinity category
- In-market segments
- Other categories
- Location
- Technology where you Segment your users' sessions by their web and mobile technologies. Includes:
  - Operating System
  - Operating System Version
  - Browser
  - Browser Version
  - Screen Resolution
  - Device Category
  - Mobile (Including Tablet)
  - Mobile Device Branding
  - Mobile Device Model
- Behaviour where you Segment your users by how often they visit and conduct transactions. Includes:
  - Sessions
  - Day since last session
  - Transactions
  - Session Duration
- Date of First Session where you Segment your users (create cohorts) by when they first visited. Includes:
  - First session date range
- Traffic Sources where you Segment your users by how they found you. Includes:
  - Campaign
  - Medium
  - Source

- Keyword
- Enhanced Ecommerce where you can Segment your users by their shopping behavior. Includes:
    - Revenue
    - Product
    - Product category
    - Product brand
    - Product variant
- Conditions where you can segment your users and/or their sessions according to single or multi-session conditions. Includes:
    - Wide variety of options between dimensions and metrics which you can use in segmentation.
- Sequences that Segment your users and/or their sessions according to sequential conditions.

I know all this might seem overwhelming yet most of the options above are rarely used, yet it is good to know them.

Most of the time filtering happens on the demographic level.

The moment you create the segments you will be able to see them on the very top of the page with a percentage sign next to each one of the segments reflecting the percentage of the total visitors that are represented in this segment. See below:

Daniel	Melissa	Mike
3.42% Users	0.28% Users	3.68% Users

You will realize that all your metrics are now divided into 4 and a color coded.

Users	New Users	Sessions	Number of Sessions per User
All Users	All Users	All Users	All Users
46,527	43,174	58,662	1.26
Daniel	Daniel	Daniel	Daniel
1,590	1,383	2,210	1.39
Melissa	Melissa	Melissa	Melissa
128	117	191	1.49
Mike	Mike	Mike	Mike
1,712	1,601	2,156	1.26

This will help you see how each of your segments are performing compared to each other and compared to the total amount of users on the site.

I always tend to keep all users there as it is a good benchmark to see if your segment is performing above or below average.

So let's say I want to see which persona has the highest conversion rate:

Looking at this graph, you can see that Daniel, from the USA is more likely to convert than the average visitor coming to the site.

Source: Google Analytics

Chapter 5

Analytics Integration

Getting the best out of Analytics.

"Installing analytics and customizing it properly without checking it regularly is like having a Ferrari in the garage and never using it." – Tarek Riman

Analytics is about acting.

Chapter 5.0. Dashboarding – Google Data Studio

Chapter 5.1. Google Analytics & SEO

Chapter 5.2. Google Analytics & Content

Chapter 5.3. Google Analytics & SEM

Chapter 5.4 Google Analytics and Social

Chapter 5.5 Google Optimizer & AB Testing

Chapter 5.0 - Dashboarding
Google Data Studio

It's one thing to set up data analytics, another to learn how to read it, and yet another to start customizing how that data shows up, and how to derive the most value from it.

With today's technology, it's possible to analyze data and extract actionable insights almost immediately – an effort that's slower and less efficient with more traditional business intelligence solutions.

But data isn't the only thing moving fast in business, and for many professionals and entrepreneurs, there just aren't enough hours in the day to have regular deep dives into the data.

This is where dashboarding becomes extremely valuable.

Regardless of whether I'm working with Fortune 500 companies or small business entrepreneurs, it is always imperative that the right data reach the right people.

As a consultant, I am often the business's SEO, SEM and Analytics agency, and I communicate with the content writing agency, the social media agency, the media buying agency, etc., so that all the data can be aggregated, assessed and acted upon.

When it comes to dashboarding and integrating all the work that we discussed, I am a proponent of Google Data Studio. Google Data Studio is a Google-owned dashboarding web tool. It helps you make your data stand out and helps inspire you to run a smarter business.

If it seems like I'm exclusively recommending Google products, I am. Google simply does analytics really well. But, on top of that, if you're going to use multiple tools or platforms, it makes sense to opt for tools produced and maintained by the same company because they typically integrate seamlessly, which you absolutely want when it comes to your data.

To get started with dashboarding, access Google Data Studio at **https://datastudio.google.com**

This fast paced, high tech, data-at-your-fingertips era we're in also means we have a whole new problem of way too much data on our hands.

Because of this, software like Data Studio will start playing bigger roles, as the issue of managing, processing and displaying data becomes increasingly important.

Intro to the Google Data Studio Dashboard

When you open Data Studio, you will be forwarded to a dashboard showing you the following templates:
- Google Analytics Dashboard Template
- Google AdWords Dashboard Template
- Google Search Console Dashboard Template
- YouTube Channel Report
- World Population Data
- Ecommerce PPC
- Google Merchandise Store
- Olympics TV Ad Performance
- Firebase Events Report
- Crashlytics Dashboard

Each of these templates will help you create a customized report from different sources of traffic, such as:
- Google Analytics
- Search Console
- Google Ads
- YouTube Analytics
- Google Sheets
- Google BigQuery

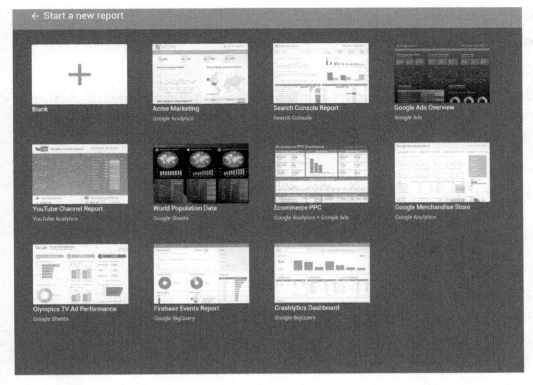

You will also see recent reports, reports owned by you, reports shared with you and deleted reports.

Getting Started

Google Analytics

Click on the Google Analytics template.

You will be shown the template with a sample report and can choose whether or not to use it.

Click "Use Template".

You will then be prompted to choose a data source.

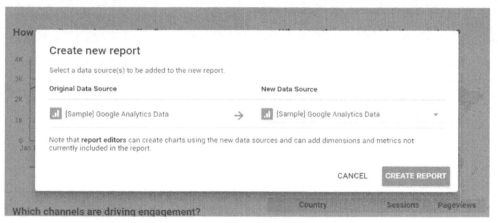

Click the "New Data Source" drop-down and select "[Sample] Google Analytics Data".

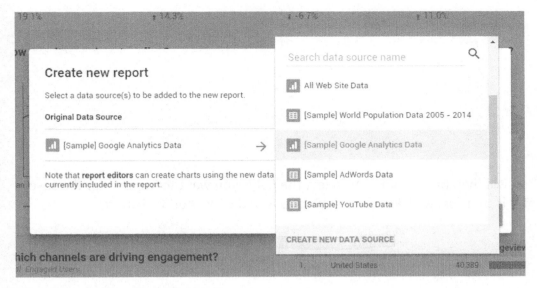

Click "Create New Data Source".

A window will pop up asking you to choose from one of the Google Connectors.

Choose Google Analytics for this exercise.

You will then be asked to authorize a connection between Google Analytics and Google Data Studio. Click "Authorize".

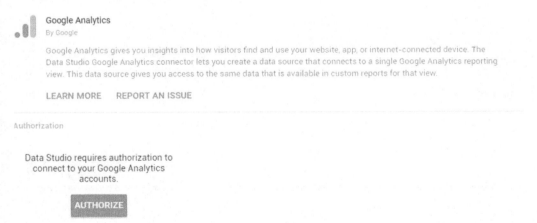

In the next window, search for the account, property and view that you want to connect. Remember back at the beginning when we talked about the importance of your GA structure and how it would come into play in various ways? This is a prime example of that importance.

You will then be prompted to select the fields you want to import. For the sake of this exercise, we'll keep everything as is and click "Add to Report".

You will then see that a new connection has been created. Click "Create Report".

Create new report

Select a data source(s) to be added to the new report.

Original Data Source		New Data Source
[Sample] Google Analytics Data	→	All Web Site Data

Note that **report editors** can create charts using the new data sources and can add dimensions and metrics not currently included in the report.

CANCEL   CREATE REPORT

The newly connected data will then show up on your new dashboard.

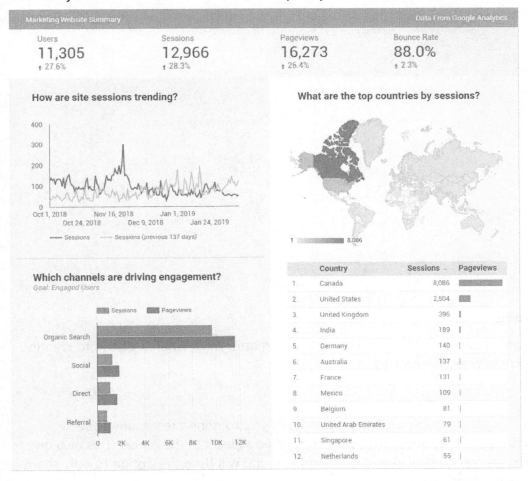

Once you're all set with the right data source, your next step is to customize how the data will appear.

To get started, let's get familiar with the dashboard.

Google Data Studio Dashboard

Tools

For this example, I'll cover the parts that matter most when it comes to creating a customized dashboard.

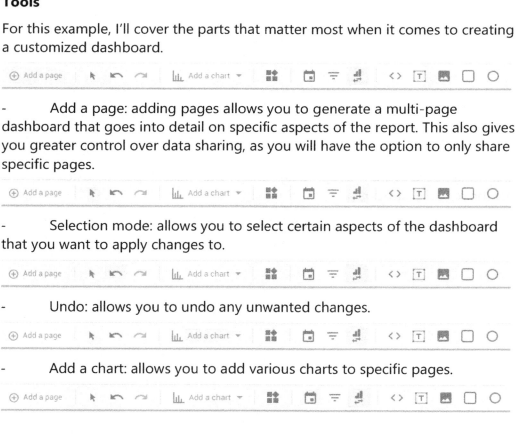

- Add a page: adding pages allows you to generate a multi-page dashboard that goes into detail on specific aspects of the report. This also gives you greater control over data sharing, as you will have the option to only share specific pages.

- Selection mode: allows you to select certain aspects of the dashboard that you want to apply changes to.

- Undo: allows you to undo any unwanted changes.

- Add a chart: allows you to add various charts to specific pages.

- Date range: allows you to add a date range option so that viewers of the dashboard can manage the date range of what they're viewing.

- Text: allows you to add plain text to the report. You can use this to add details, descriptions, section titles, or other notations.

- Embed a URL: allows you to embed a view of a specific web page.

- Image: allows you to add images to the report.

- The rectangle and circle icons are for aesthetic purposes, allowing you to adjust the look and feel of your report.

Side bars (part 1)

Layout

Layout is applied to the entire report. You will only have the option to edit the layout when no specific report section is selected.

Layout allows you to customize the look and feel of your report and is entirely a question of preference.

I usually choose the following settings:

-        Header Visibility: Autohide

-        Display Mode: Actual Size

-        Has Margin

-        Canvas size: US letter

-        Grid Setting: 50 (allows me to divide the page in an easy-to-consume way)

You can play around with these settings. Have fun, make your report unique, but do keep clarity in mind. You will likely spend a lot of time looking at these reports, so ensure they are easy on the eyes and easy to read.

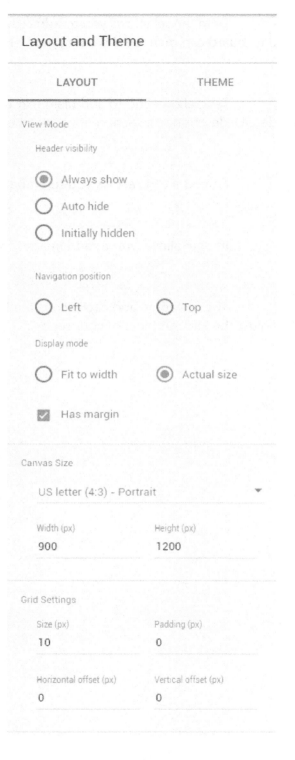

Side bars (part 2)

Theme

After working on your layout, you can set a theme.

This is another opportunity to brand your reports and make them look unique.

I usually choose the colour of my own brand, or the brand colours of the client, and customize it visually.

This may seem frivolous, but even in reporting, I've found that first impressions matter. People are usually more impressed by how things look (at least at first), than by how they are. By aligning a report with the branding and look and feel of the business, you may also feel greater ownership of your data. And, let's face it. Data reporting can feel a bit dry. Why not dress it up?

That being said, do choose your report theme carefully, as it will go a long way.

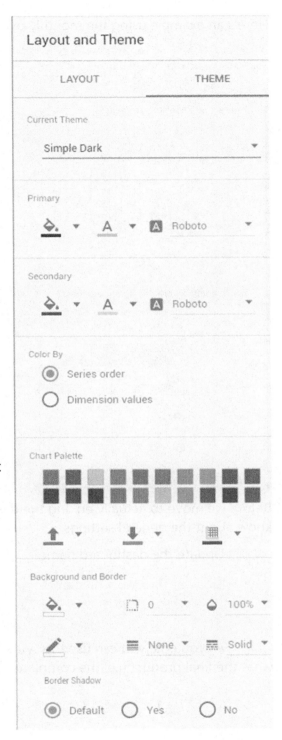

Here's an example using the monthly overview report of my site, Montreal Tips:

Before we move to actually editing the dashboard, there are a few things to know about the general settings.

- Update the dashboard name.

- As you edit, you can use the "View" button at the top of the page to see what the final product (i.e. the completed dashboard) will look like.

- You have the option to download the dashboard in different formats.

-        You have the option of embedding the report on a website, which can come in especially handy if your business uses intranet.

-        You can toggle the report to full screen.

-        You can refresh the report to ensure you have the absolute most up to date data.

-        You can duplicate the report.

That last option is particularly helpful when you are making a lot of changes to the report and want to keep an older version as a backup.

Editing Reports in Google Data Studio

To start making edits to a specific graph, all you have to do is click on the graph.

Once you click the graph, the sidebar will automatically change to show both the data and style aspects of the report, which you can then edit.

The data sidebar allows you to update what you see in the report window.

In this example, you can see that we are measuring the number of visitors across a certain period of time. So, the dimension is 'date' and the metric is 'user sessions'.

From the sidebar, you can update these metrics and dimensions to pull in the data you need.

For example, if we want to see how many views of our ads occurred vs. the number of visits that occurred with a search on site, all we need to do is click on the metrics section to update and add the metric.

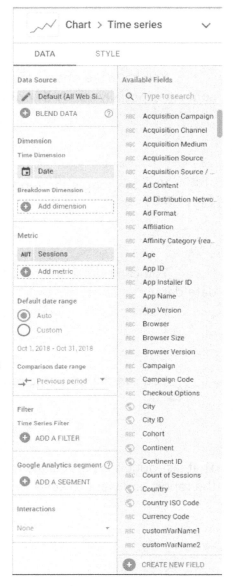

Here is the updated report based on the new dimensions mentioned before:

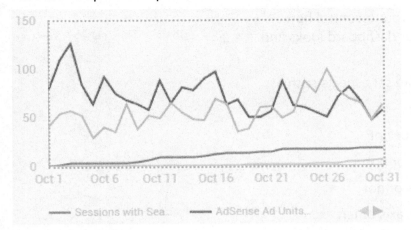

My second favourite feature under the data sidebar is the filter.

Using filters allows you to send different dashboards to different agencies or groups of people without creating individual dashboards for each. This keeps your digital clutter to a minimum.

Let's say, for example, we want to send an SEO report to the SEO team.

We click on filters and create a new filter, as shown below. The report will update to show only the traffic coming from organic search. We can then share just that report with the SEO team.

You can do similar filters with segments, where you segment traffic based on added segments, system segments or custom segments.

Report Style

Report style allows you to control how every report on your dashboard looks and feels.

This is where you can set aspects such as:

- Lines vs. bars

- Cumulative or not

- Show labels or not

- Show points or not

- Have a right axis or left axis

- Have a trendline

- Customize how the axis, grid, and the legend look

Takeaway

Best Practices for Google Data Studio:

Clearly name your pages on Google Dashboard to help you navigate easily.

If you are creating multiple pages, it's easiest to duplicate the original, then customize.

Remember that Google Data Studio doesn't impact the data itself. What it does is make it look aesthetically pleasing, more meaningful and easier to consume. That matters a lot.

Cluttered data equals a cluttered mind, so remember to practice good data hygiene. Less is more. If you don't need that additional dashboard you created, delete it. If you aren't using that sixth graph, get rid of it. It's easier to see, analyze and act on the most valuable data if it isn't hiding in a haystack of irrelevant graphs, images and other elements.

We just scratched the surface here, but I urge you to get on Google Data Studio and start discovering it on your own. Don't be afraid to make mistakes. That's how we learn.

Exercise

Go to the Google Analytics Demo Account.

https://datastudio.google.com

Complete the following exercises:

- Create your dashboard.
- Choose a data source.
- Customize the report to bring forward the most relevant results.

Chapter 5.1 - Google Analytics & SEO

How to Use Google Analytics to Improve Your Site's SEO Presence

The mission of search engines

The role of search engines is to crawl the web and index the pages that they deem worthy, in an order that provides value to users.

In doing so, their mission is to ensure users can quickly and easily find the information, products, services or content they're looking for.

Google's mission statement, written in 2013, is as follows: "Google's mission is to organize the world's information and make it universally accessible and useful."

Source: *https://www.google.com/about/*

Bing's mission statement, also written in 2013, is as follows: "At Bing our central mission is to help you search less and do more. To that end, we're constantly looking for ways to make your search experience more efficient."

Source: https://blogs.bing.com/search/2013/08/23/find-it-faster-with-bing-product-search/

Yahoo's mission is to "make the world's daily habits inspiring and entertaining."

Source: Yahoo.com

What can we take away from this?

Essentially, search engines exist to send us *away* from them and *to* what users search for. Ironic, isn't it?

Think about it. You visit a search engine, perform a search and then leave. The better the experience you have with a search engine (i.e. The greater success you have at finding what you want), the more likely you are to use that one again. With that in mind, you can rely on them wanting to return search results that are as closely related as possible to what it "thinks" you are truly looking for.

There is a lot to learn from this.

My grandpa used to say, "Tell me what someone wants and I will tell you how to control him." And I tell you today that if you want to control how your web property shows up in search engines, you have to understand that the primary mission of the search engine is around what people want and nothing else. Yes, the companies behind them want to make money through advertising, sales, etc., but they know that these things are most profitable when driven by that primary mission of providing value.

User-driven metrics control search, and likely always will.

If you are able, through your site, to provide useful, accessible, engaging, inspiring and entertaining information, then you are golden. If people want you, search engines will want you. This should be the guiding principle behind your SEO strategy.

Thankfully, GA can help you understand what searchers want, like, enjoy, engage with and how you can act on that knowledge to improve your ranking.

Google Search Console on Google Analytics

Going back to chapter 14, where we installed Google Search Console, you may recall that GA alone is not enough for us to capture adequate data to take a knowledge-driven approach to SEO.

To be able to make educated SEO decisions, you need Google Search Console. Once you connect Google Search Console data to your web property, you will have access to a wide array of reports that will help you understand how pages are performing, what keywords are sending the most traffic, what pages are getting the highest engagement, what is relevant and what is not.

The goal of this chapter is to help you capitalize on GA to optimize your site's organic search performance in the best way possible.

Let's jump back to the GA dashboard.

Under "Acquisition" scroll to "Search Console".

Without Google Search Console, the default analytics results are extremely limited. In fact, GA will often return "Not Provided".

With Search Console, you will have access to extensive data, which is enough to optimize, improve and plan ahead.

.ıl Analytics   All accounts > Montreal Tips
    All Web Site Data ▾

🏠 Home

▪▪ Customization

REPORTS

🕓 Real-Time

👤 Audience

⤳ Acquisition

    Overview

   ▾ All Traffic

   ▾ Google Ads

   ▲ Search Console

     Landing Pages

     Countries

     Devices

     Queries

   ▾ Social

   ▾ Campaigns

▭ Behavior

⚑ Conversions

Also, Google Search Console is the best SEO tool out there that you can use for free. Make sure that you are using it and learning from it as much as possible.

Search Console Landing Pages Report

Landing Page	Acquisition						Behavior		Conversion: Goal 1: Engaged Visitors ▾		
	Impressions ↓	Clicks	CTR	Average Position	Sessions	Bounce Rate	Pages / Sessions	Engaged Visitors (Goal 1 Completions)	Engaged Visitors (Goal 1 Value)	Engaged Visitors (Goal 1 Conversion Rate)
	72,718	3,584	4.93%	25	987	91.29%	1.23	29	CA$0.00	2.94%
	12,506	586	4.34%	30	203	93.10%	1.11	4	CA$0.00	1.97%
	12,350	578	4.68%	14	0	0.00%	0.00	0	CA$0.00	0.00%
	6,032	342	4.81%	35	96	93.75%	1.11	4	CA$0.00	4.17%
	3,904	76	1.95%	3.9	0	0.00%	0.00	0	CA$0.00	0.00%
	3,705	274	7.40%	25	152	92.76%	1.12	4	CA$0.00	2.63%

As you can see in the report above, GA provides a list of the most popular landing pages on your site that visitors have arrived at through organic search.

The table shows a lot of valuable info, which is the result of the merge between Google Search Console data and on-site behaviour data. This helps you not only know what people did to find your page, but what they did once they arrived there, and whether they took the actions that you want them to take.

These are the terms you should know to get the most out of this report:

SERP (Search Engine Results Page) Impressions – This is the number of times your pages popped up in search results.

Clicks – The number of times people clicked on your page from an SERP.

CTR (Click Through Rate) – The number of clicks/the number of impressions * 100, meaning, it reflects the rate at which people see your listing in organic search results and choose to click through to your site.

Average Position – This is the average ranking of your page in organic search results, taking into account all the keywords that this page ranks for. If your page has an average position of 3, for example, that means your page usually shows up around the third spot in SERPs (which is a very good position to have).

Sessions – This is the number of visits that you get to your site from organic search.

Bounce Rate – This tells you how many visitors to your site (from organic search) left without taking any action.

Goal Metrics – This shows how your traffic from organic search is converting on the site.

The Landing Page Report gives you a view into how your different pages are performing from an SEO perspective. It helps you see what pages are performing well, which ones can be improved, and which pages you can capitalize on elsewhere, maybe through paid search or social campaigns.

Acquisition Google Search Console Countries Report

| Country | Acquisition | | | | B |
	Impressions ↓	Clicks	CTR	Average Position	Sessions
	72,718 % of Total: 100.00% (72,718)	3,584 % of Total: 100.00% (3,584)	4.93% Avg for View: 4.93% (0.00%)	25 Avg for View: 25 (0.00%)	987 % of Total: 29.52% (3,344)
1. Canada	32,229 (44.32%)	1,991 (55.55%)	6.18%	14	500 (50.66%)
2. United States	12,661 (17.41%)	838 (23.38%)	6.62%	17	242 (24.52%)
3. India	3,828 (5.26%)	75 (2.09%)	1.96%	48	14 (1.42%)
4. United Kingdom	2,791 (3.84%)	197 (5.50%)	7.06%	18	60 (6.08%)
5. Brazil	1,250 (1.72%)	6 (0.17%)	0.48%	54	2 (0.20%)
6. Indonesia	1,022 (1.41%)	2 (0.06%)	0.20%	56	2 (0.20%)
7. France	915 (1.26%)	33 (0.92%)	3.61%	39	10 (1.01%)
8. Russia	900 (1.24%)	3 (0.08%)	0.33%	56	0 (0.00%)
9. Vietnam	875 (1.20%)	4 (0.11%)	0.46%	57	0 (0.00%)
10. Mexico	847 (1.16%)	17 (0.47%)	2.01%	37	10 (1.01%)

In this report, you can see the amount of organic search traffic you're getting from each country.

This insight can help you tailor future content for different countries, with different languages and different information that caters to specific audiences.

I use this report to understand who is coming to my site and how I can tailor new content for them. It also helps me identify opportunities I may be missing out on. For example, if I'm getting a lot of traffic from a specific country, but it isn't converting, I can start looking into why that may be, and what I can do to better serve that traffic and increase conversions.

In the sample report above, you can see that the US is the second-biggest source of traffic to my site. Because of that, I try to tailor some content to that audience instead of only concentrating on Canadian traffic or local traffic.

Acquisition Google Search Console Device Report

Device Category	Acquisition				
	Impressions ↓	Clicks	CTR	Average Position	Sessions
	72,718 % of Total: 100.00% (72,718)	3,584 % of Total: 100.00% (3,584)	4.93% Avg for View: 4.93% (0.00%)	25 Avg for View: 25 (0.00%)	987 % of Total: 29.52% (3,344)
1. desktop	36,241 (49.84%)	1,507 (42.05%)	4.16%	37	758 (76.80%)
2. mobile	33,794 (46.47%)	1,846 (51.51%)	5.46%	13	95 (9.63%)
3. tablet	2,683 (3.69%)	231 (6.45%)	8.61%	8.9	134 (13.58%)

As small as this report is, it packs a big punch.

This gives you a quick overview of where you stand as a brand and site, as it shows your average position on mobile, tablet and desktop.

If you see that you have a lower than usual CTR on mobile, for example, it may be a sign that you are not appealing to users of these devices. You may find that you need to do a better job with meta title and meta descriptions, or even that your site isn't rendering properly on mobile devices.

Acquisition Google Search Console Queries Report

Search Query	Clicks	Impressions	CTR	Average Position
	1,406	44,036	3.19%	32
1. national parks near montreal	123	373	32.98%	1.9
2. montreal national park	60	196	30.61%	1.9
3. national park near montreal	57	119	47.90%	1.5
4. indoor activities montreal	47	730	6.44%	7.0
5. montreal indoor activities	40	368	10.87%	5.2
6. montreal national parks	35	99	35.36%	1.7
7. national park montreal	28	66	42.42%	1.5
8. indoor activities in montreal	23	136	16.91%	4.3
9. best national parks near montreal	21	39	53.85%	1.3
10. canadian winter jackets brands	21	597	3.52%	11

This report is, for SEO purposes, the most important one in the Google Search Console reports, as it shows what terms and keywords visitors used to arrive on your site.

This shows what you're good at and what you can improve, in terms of keywords.

It is a great place to see what type of content to concentrate on more, and gives you the start of a model for how to approach future content and what types of terms to concentrate on for a more targeted and sustained approach to the details on your site.

Takeaway

GA, in partnership with Google Search Console, helps you understand how visitors search for your site, how they perceive it and if they find it relevant, giving you a starting point from which to build and improve on your content strategy for better SEO.

What makes GA so important as a tool, is that it taps into user metrics, and these user metrics are the main ranking factors of any website, as of this writing.

Exercise

Go to the Google Analytics Demo Account.

https://analytics.google.com/analytics/web/demoAccount

Complete the following exercises:

- Identify the terms driving the most organic traffic.
- Identify the terms driving the highest engagement.
- Identify the terms leading to the highest bounce rate.
- Identify the terms leading to the most conversions.
- Determine the average ranking position for branded terms (a branded term is one that includes the business or brand name).
- Identify the best performing landing page for organic traffic.

By extracting the information above, you will begin to build a picture of what is working, what is relevant and what should be optimized.

Chapter 5.2 - Google Analytics & Content

How to Use Google Analytics to Create Better Content

Are You Missing the Boat on Data-Driven Content Marketing?

Do you want high performing content? We all want that!

In working with a variety of companies, from small startups to Fortune 500s, I've learned that analytics is a tool not capitalized on enough, especially when it comes to content marketing. Even big companies, with huge marketing budgets, are missing the boat.

Interestingly, analytics tends to be looked at only *after* a paid campaign, end of the season, or before the end of the year. Sadly, most companies don't even consider looking at data pre-campaign, which is a huge missed opportunity.

The more I work with analytics, the more I realize how necessary a research and study tool it is and that it should be considered in all phases of a campaign, especially when it comes to content marketing.

Why? Because analytics doesn't just tell you what worked, it can also help you predict what will work in the future and what to use to make it work... if you look in the right place!

That's why, when the time arrives to create relevant, engaging content, I look to five main GA metrics. A good grasp of these metrics is like a crystal ball view into giving users more of what they want.

- **Site Content**

In GA, just under "Site Content", you can see the pages on your site that get the most visits. This provides insight into your most popular topics or content types, allowing you to predict the topics and formats that are most engaging and appealing to your visitors.

Look at your bounce rates, exits and average time on page.

With this data, you will be able to plan future content either by using similar content structure, similar topics, or even just a similar general approach.

- **Site Search**

If you have site search capabilities built-in, Site Search metrics is the best way to see what people look for once they arrive on your site.

Are people searching for something you don't have a lot of content on? Or maybe you do, but they're using different terms and not finding what you have?

Remember, knowing what people are looking for is like having a crystal ball, telling you what content to create or enhance.

This can tell you how to cater to new visitors, align your content strategy with current customer needs, and know what content to use in ads and promotions.

- **Audience Details**

What types of people are visiting your site? This can help you determine the type of content to deliver. For example, you may discover you have a large millennial or baby boomer audience you can tailor content to. Perhaps you have high traffic from a particular country and you can adjust some existing content to have a more local flair.

When it comes to audience details, there can be many factors to consider.

To make better sense of the numbers, I usually look at at least 3 months of data to get more content-worthy metrics, and look at these key metrics:

1. Demographics (age and gender)

2. Interests (affinity categories and in-market segments) - Helps me understand the general and related interests that my visitors have, allowing me to create better content and target them in my social or search campaigns.

3. Geo (language and location) - Pay close attention to language. Over time, you may notice a growing traffic segment associated with another language, or that there is potential for expanding your market.

Having this demographic knowledge will help you create the right content, for the right age group, at the right place, at the right time.

- **Channels**

'Acquisition' is the way in which you acquire visitors. 'Channels' refers to your acquisition channels - the sources driving visitors. This is where you will find the top sources of traffic to your site. For example, you can acquire visitors from Google, referrals from other sites, article mentions, newsletters and more.

Knowing how you got your current visitors will help you understand how your content is being shared, searched and viewed, and which content is best at drawing people in.

Knowing this empowers you to create content catered to the different visitors in your different channels, and create even more of the type of content that is best at bringing new visitors to your site.

- **Search Console**

Under 'Acquisition' in GA is where you'll find your Search Console data, which, as previously discussed, is only functional when you link GA with Google Search Console.

From Search Console, you can see which keywords or queries in Google are leading people to your site. You will also see how well you rank for these keywords, and the number of impressions you get for them.

This data will allow you to assess what is working as far as search goes, help you further capitalize on these topics, and empower you to work on better and more relevant content for your site.

Takeaway

Analytics can be a big part of creating great content. Taking advantage of analytics BEFORE creating or modifying content makes it part of a truly powerful cycle of creating content, seeing how it works on your web properties and sites, realigning your content strategy in accordance with the data gathered, and back to creating content. The big difference being, your content gets better, more relevant and more engaging each time.

Make sure you are using GA to its fullest potential to maximize your advantages. Always check your data and analytics before planning strategies or campaigns. Listen to what they are telling you. Make them an essential part of your overall marketing strategy and you will begin to see your content performing better than ever before.

Exercise:

Using the personas that you created in the Google Audience Report exercise, it's time to create content! Write one paragraph for each persona that aligns fully with the persona details.

For the sake of this exercise, assume that you are selling Google merchandise on the Google Merchandise store.

https://www.googlemerchandisestore.com/

If you're finding it difficult to write for the personas you created, resist the urge to create new personas. In the real world, you get the visitors you get. Consider this good practise and a valuable workout for your creative muscles.

Chapter 5.3 - Google Analytics & SEM

How to capitalize on Google analytics as part of your search engine marketing approach and strategy?

SEM Stands for Search Engine Marketing.

Both SEO and SEM fall under the search marketing umbrella. SEO is the organic traffic and SEM is the paid traffic.

The tools that most advertisers use to run SEM campaigns are Google Ads and Bing Ads.

For the sake of this book, we will take a peek into how Google Ads works with Google Analytics, highlight the value of these two tools working together, and explore how to use the resulting reports and data.

One big benefit of using GA is that it is easily integrated with other Google tools. As mentioned earlier, this seamless integration is a big advantage when it comes to data.

Google Ads is by far one of the most superior tools when it comes to creating search, video and display campaigns. Yet, on its own, it's not enough.

Any marketer with knowledge of the ad industry will tell you that without integrating Google Ads with Google Analytics, you can't fully capitalize on the tool.

Alone, Google Ads can give you insight into how users are performing before they arrive on your site, but the moment they arrive on your site, Google Ads tracking is done. That's where you want Analytics to pick up the thread, as it is critical to understand what your ad traffic does post-click. This is how you know whether or not the investments you're making are worth it.

Integrating GA with Google Ads will allow you to get the full picture so that you can respond accordingly.

To get started, we need to connect our GA account with Google Ads.

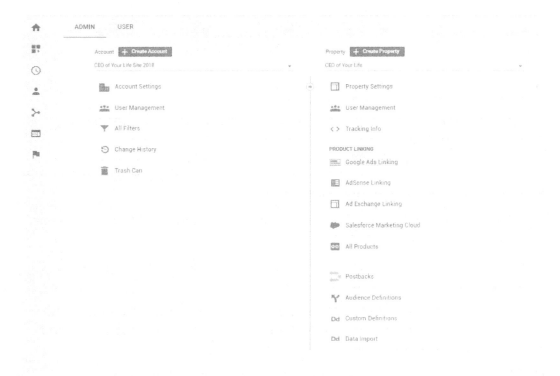

Go to Admin in your GA account. Under "Property" select "Google Ads Linking". You'll then get a window asking you to add a new link group.

Google Ads Linking

Click "New Link Group" and a window will pop up showing you all the Google Ads accounts you are running under your associated Gmail account (remember that it all starts with a Gmail address).

If you are running a Google Ads account under another Gmail address, it might be best to transfer ownership so that you can make the connection.

Configure Google Ads link group

By linking your Analytics property to your Google Ads account(s), you will enable data to flow between the products. Data exported from your Analytics property into Google Ads is subject to the Google Ads terms of service, while Google Ads data imported into Analytics is subject to the Analytics terms of service. Learn more

Select linked Google Ads accounts

Select the account you want to connect and click "Continue".

You will then be asked to add a link group title, connect to a specific view and hit "Save".

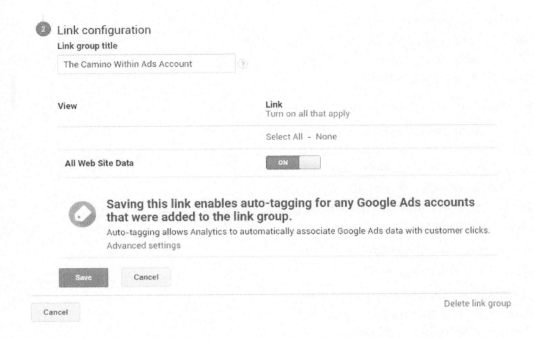

This connection will bring a lot of benefits, whether it's the more in-depth reporting from the Google Analytics side of things, or the ability to customize your bidding and targeting based on the data that you are extracting to Google Ads.

So, if we go to the main analytics report section in GA, click on "Acquisition" and scroll to "Google Ads", a drop-down will show up.

Here's what to pay attention to:

-       Accounts: This report shows you how your account is performing and, if you have more than one account connected, it will allow you to see how the accounts are performing compared to each other.

For most of the companies I work with, there is usually one account.

The main benefit of this report is that you are able to see the performance of the whole account in one place. Meaning, if there is any drop, spike, or problem, it is easy to pinpoint.

Also, this report gives you a quick idea of whether your investment is worth it and if you might want to invest more, depending on your budget.

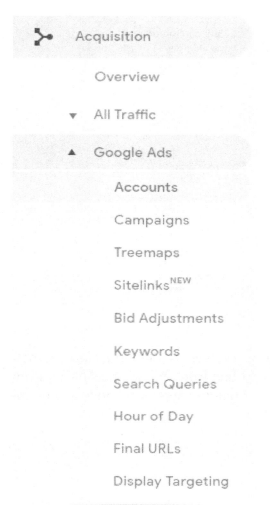

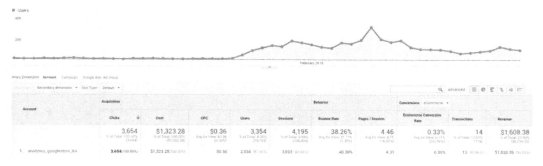

The reason I say this is due to the fact that you can see clicks, visits, behaviour and conversions all in one place.

-       The second tab to look at is the Campaigns tab.

This tab allows you to see how your campaigns are performing, how visitors to the site are behaving and whether they are converting.

- The Sitelinks tab is another great report as it gives an in-depth look into which sitelinks on your Google Ads account are the best performers, and what you can improve on.

When I look at this report, I'm typically searching for the most successful terms and calls to action, which I then use to improve any ads that are underperforming or not converting well.

- Bid Adjustments report.

A bid adjustment is when you alter your bid for certain factors in your Ads account.

One of these factors could be devices (Mobile, Computer or Tablet). Let's say you adjust your bid for a 10% increase on mobile. As you would expect, this increase should (ideally) lead to an increase in leads, impressions and clicks.

A bid adjustment can be either negative or positive. For example, I could set a bid adjustment of -10% for tablets, meaning we would likely see a drop in tablet ad impressions of about 10%.

Campaign	Device	Bid Adj.	Acquisition			Behavior				Conversions eCommerce		
			Clicks	Cost	CPC	Users	Sessions	Bounce Rate	Pages / Session	Ecommerce Conversion Rate	Transactions	Revenue
	ALL	--	3,654 % of Total: 100.00% (3,654)	$1,323.28 % of Total: 100.00% ($1,323.28)	$0.36 Avg for View: $0.36 (0.00%)	2,934 % of Total: 3.73% (78,763)	3,593 % of Total: 3.41% (105,494)	40.30% Avg for View: 37.17% (8.71%)	4.31 Avg for View: 4.75 (-9.27%)	0.36% Avg for View: 0.15% (225.00%)	13 % of Total: 11.21% (116)	$1,528.39 % of Total: 22.71% ($6,729.10)
1. AW - Apparel	ALL	--	1,966	$990.53	$0.25	1,244	1,617	27.83%	5.42	0.56%	4	$1,277.61
	Computers	--	958	$327.83	$0.38	688	873	27.21%	9.35	0.23%	2	$64.93
	Mobile devices with full browsers	--	660	$86.85	$0.09	521	755	29.07%	6.40	0.85%	6	$1,183.97
	Tablets with full browsers	--	48	$2.85	$0.06	36	42	20.93%	7.28	2.33%	1	$61.77
2. AW - YouTube	ALL	--	1,355	$678.44	$0.50	1,190	1,175	62.81%	2.17	0.00%	0	$0.00
3. AW - Google Brand	ALL	--	321	$101.91	$0.32	273	365	30.16%	4.39	0.95%	7	$94.68

The Bid Adjustment report helps you see whether the adjustments you make are yielding better results or leading to a higher ROI. And, if not, it might be a good idea to revisit the bid adjustment that you set up in the first place.

- Keywords and Search Queries reports are two different reports. The Keywords report shows you which keywords you input into Google Ads and how they are performing. The Search Queries report shows you the keywords used by search engine users that led them to your site or web property.

- Final URL Report is a great one to look at. This shows you which of your landing pages are performing best. You can act on that insight by using your top performing landing pages more often, or by taking elements of your successful landing pages and repeating them on others to improve their performance.

- Hours of the Day Report shows you the best performing hours of the day. This is helpful because time of day is one of the metrics you can set when setting up your bids. Ideally, you want to concentrate your investment on the hours that perform best for you.

Google Ads

Google Analytics and Google Ads, when used together, have even more benefits you can tap into from the Google Ads side.

- **Goals and Conversions.**

When connecting the two accounts together, you will be able to import your goals from Google Analytics into Google AdWords, meaning you will be able to optimize your campaigns to goals and acquisitions, vs. just clicks and impressions.

- **CPA– Cost per acquisition**

When you have AdWords connected to Analytics, you will be able to start using the CPA bidding strategy, instead of just CPC (Cost Per Click) and CPM (Cost per 1000 Impressions). This matters because while clicks and impressions are important to measure, whether or not those clicks and impressions lead to actual visits matters more.

- **Audiences & Remarketing**

Google Analytics allows you to create audiences that you can then target in your Google Ads. Here's how you set it up:

- Go to the admin section in GA.

- Under "Property", click on "Audience Definitions", then "Audiences".

- This is where you can create an audience, then export it to your Google Ads account, where you can target a specific group of users, with specific ads. (This is also called remarketing.)

To create the audience:

- Click "New Audience" under the audience settings.

- Select the view that you want to create the audience under and click "Next".

Audiences

Create audiences to engage with your users through Google's Audience marketing integrations, like Remarketing Lists for Search Ads and Remarketing on the Google Display Network, or with users who return to your site with Google Optimize 360. Learn More

Audience source
View
All Web Site Data

Next step   Cancel

- Click "Create New" and an audience creation window will pop up, allowing you to filter out an audience you want to target. See example below:

-        Click "Apply" and you will be prompted to name the audience. Name it something relevant as you will use it on Google Ads later. Click "Next Step".

-        The last step is to choose where you want to publish this audience. I recommend choosing Google Analytics and Google Ads.

This will help you see the performance of the audience on both Google Analytics and Google Ads. Keep in mind that "Publish" does not mean you're making anything public. It just means you're granting access to the tools you choose - in this example, GA and Google Ads - so that you will be able to see the data and reporting in those tools.

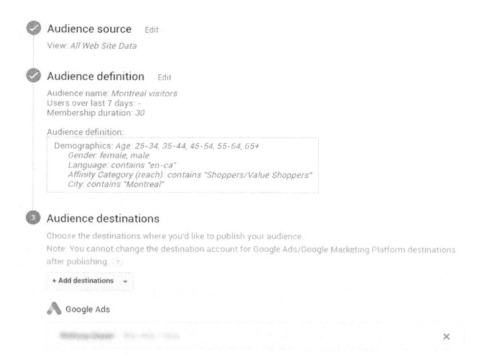

Takeaway

Google Analytics and Google Ads can be fully integrated, which provides you with incredibly valuable and actionable insights. Make sure you are capitalizing on this integration from both tools.

Exercise:

Connect your Google Analytics account to your Google AdWords account.

Create an audience in GA and export it to Google Ads.

Chapter 5.4 - Google Analytics and Social

How to use Google Analytics to improve social media tracking and strategy?

We now come to a weakness of Google Analytics. The default social channel performance tracking in GA is not the best. Most of the time, it is hard to get an exact gauge of the amount of traffic coming from these channels.

However, a strength of Google's is providing workarounds. Having worked with many social campaigns in the past, I've realized that there is a safe way to get the exact amount of traffic from each channel, link, post or even share. It's through UTM tagging, which was briefly mentioned earlier in this book.

A UTM tag or code is a simple bit of code that you attach to a custom URL in order to track a source, medium, and campaign name. Having this tag will help you identify how every specific URL is performing on your site.

To build your own UTM tags go to https://ga-dev-tools.appspot.com/campaign-url-builder/

* Website URL	https://thecaminowithin.com/
	The full website URL (e.g. `https://www.example.com`)
* Campaign Source	Facebook
	The referrer: (e.g. `google`, `newsletter`)
Campaign Medium	summer
	Marketing medium: (e.g. `cpc`, `banner`, `email`)
Campaign Name	2019
	Product, promo code, or slogan (e.g. `spring_sale`)
Campaign Term	
	Identify the paid keywords
Campaign Content	
	Use to differentiate ads

Share the generated campaign URL

Use this URL in any promotional channels you want to be associated with this custom campaign

https://thecaminowithin.com/?utm_source=Facebook&utm_medium=summer&utm_campaign=2019

☐ Set the campaign parameters in the fragment portion of the URL (not recommended).

Use the URL exactly as generated and you will be able to easily track its performance under the Acquisition Campaign – All Campaigns report.

Source / Medium	Acquisition			Behavior
	Users	New Users	Sessions	Bounce Rate
	33,621 % of Total: 6.37% (527,892)	28,755 % of Total: 5.60% (513,634)	41,824 % of Total: 5.48% (763,906)	48.64% Avg for View: 41.52% (17.13%)
1. Partners / affiliate	20,832 (61.70%)	17,362 (60.38%)	25,165 (60.17%)	47.76%
2. google / cpc	12,921 (38.27%)	11,385 (39.59%)	16,646 (39.80%)	49.94%
3. (direct) / cpm	8 (0.02%)	8 (0.03%)	13 (0.03%)	76.92%

Especially when working on bigger campaigns, this will make tracking and reporting an easier and more efficient process. I suggest creating a formula in an Excel sheet that can automatically do the work for you.

When creating a UTM tag, pay careful attention to how you name the campaign, as you will want to be absolutely clear on what it is when checking reports. Let's say you're running a spring campaign on Facebook. Something like "FB Spring 2019" would be good. If you're planning multiple Facebook campaigns, add another descriptor such as "FB Spring 2019 coupon code" to help you immediately differentiate your campaigns.

Takeaway

When it comes to social channels and GA, don't leave data collecting on default. Make sure that you are appropriately tagging every link you use in your social campaigns.

Exercise

Create a list of UTM tagged URLs for all the site links you use in the bios or about fields of your social channels. This will help you see how much traffic you are getting from these specific links.

Chapter 5.5 - Google Optimizer & AB Testing

Testing is part of every successful marketing strategy, how can you make the best of it?

I said this at the beginning of the book and, nearing the end, I'll say it again. In marketing, ⅔ of your efforts should be focused on analytics.

The first part of this is research (preparation), the second is implementing (practice) and the third is reporting & testing (for optimal performance).

Google Optimizer is what you will use for testing. It is the best way to see and test what is working and what is not working, so that you can optimize accordingly.

"Engage your website visitors like never before. Create personalized experiences and test what works best — for free."

-        Google Optimize

To get started with Google Optimizer, go to:

https://marketingplatform.google.com/about/optimize/

You will be sent to the Google Optimizer Dashboard, where you click "Create Experience".

Experience means the journey you are creating for the visitors to interact with. It is the overall experience that you'll be testing.

Once you click "Create", a new experience sidebar will pop up:

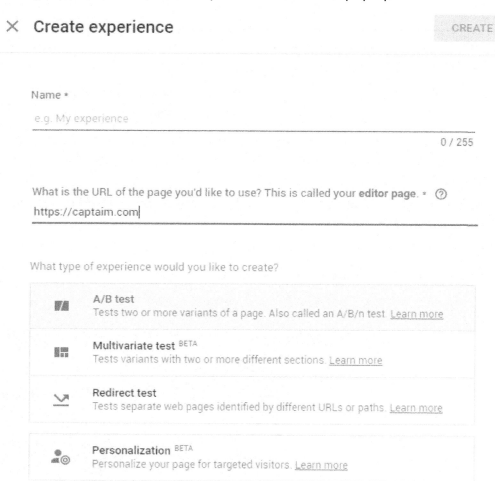

To start:

First step: Enter the name of the experience you want to create.

- Be descriptive and specific as you will be creating a lot of these experiences in the future.

- As a best practice, I tend to include the start date, the purpose and the type of experience. For example, "21st March 2019 Cap.TaiM – Redirect Test".

The second step is to add your URL. This is the URL of the page that you want to use for this experiment. In this example, I'm using my homepage, https://captaim.com

The third step is to specify which type of experiment you want to run.

- **A/B Test** - Tests two or more variants of a page. Also called an A/B/n test.
- **Multivariate test** - Tests variants with two or more different sections.
- **Redirect Test** - Tests separate web pages identified by different URLs or paths.
- **Personalization** - Personalize your page for targeted visitors.

Source: Google Optimizer: https://optimize.google.com/

For this example, I will choose the redirect test. This is perfect for testing things like which contact page will work best, to see if it is better to send people to your workshop page or book page, or some other similar test.

For this example, I will be testing my workshop page vs. my book page to see which will perform best:

https://captaim.com/workshops/ or **https://captaim.com/book/**

To get started, choose the variant.

The two pages I am testing are each a variant in the test, so I will create one variant for each, as well as my original, which is my homepage:

× Add variant   **DONE**

Variant name *
Book Page

9 / 255

Redirect destination *
https://captaim.com/book/

Final URL
https://captaim.com/**book/**

Original URL
https://captaim.com

As you can see, all the variants have been added:

I'll next add a description:

Edit experience description   **DONE**

Description
Test for month of March & April.

32 / 5000

Optimize

⤴ Measurement and objectives

▪ Google Analytics

Optimize uses Google Analytics for measurement.

Link to your Google Analytics property to enable measurement.

LINK TO ANALYTICS

⚑ Objectives ⑦

The website functionality you wish to optimize. Learn more

Before adding objectives, you need to link this container and experience to Analytics.

There isn't much point in running a test if we can't analyze results, so my next step is to connect Google Optimize with GA.

I will also activate email notifications to receive the most important and relevant updates.

When all is set, I'll click "Start" to kick off the experiment.

Takeaway

Testing is essential to know what is working, what is not and where to make changes or adjustments.

Make sure to tap into the different types of testing that Google provides and make sure that you are using them to your advantage.

Exercise

Create a Google Optimizer Account and launch an experiment that you deem relevant for your business. Don't forget to connect it to GA.

Analytics Questions for Every Business.

Is Your Business Taking FULL Advantage of Data & Analytics?

Almost every business today has a web presence, and almost all of them have some form of data and analytics setup to measure the activity and/or effectiveness of that presence.

But, are you getting the FULL picture?

In my time working with entrepreneurs and small businesses, all the way up to Fortune 500s, I have come across far too many businesses that don't take full advantage of analytics. Often, they aren't even fully aware of what analytics can do.

The result? Missed opportunity after missed opportunity, competitors getting ahead, wasted resources and frustrated leaders wondering what piece of the ever-growing digital puzzle they're missing.

The most frustrating part is that getting fully up to speed on data and analytics is not a roadblock at all. It's surprisingly easy to overcome and doesn't require a technical background.

When you and/or your team master data and analytics, you are able to:

- Identify where visitors are coming from
    - Which channels are sending the highest-converting visitors
    - Where to invest more resources to increase quality traffic
    - Where to cut resources
    - Missed localization opportunities
    - Partnership or advertising opportunities with high potential
- See what visitors are doing once they arrive on your web property
    - Map your various customer acquisition funnels

- o   See where people drop off so you can plug the leak
- o   Identify the pages with the highest conversion rates
- o   Identify important "under the radar" pages (for example, you may have an extremely low-converting page, but discover that it consistently sends high-converting visitors to your highest converting page)

- Test practically every element of your pages and properties
  - o   Which landing page converts best? What button colour gets clicked more? Do videos or images convert better? Best font? Best link text? Best menu style? Test. All. Of. It.

- Identify hidden opportunities during your off-season
  - o   Holiday or gift-giving cycles you may be missing out on
  - o   Opportunities to strengthen page rank in preparation for stronger high seasons
  - o   Branding opportunities to stay top-of-mind year-round

- Build a data-driven content strategy
  - o   Identify growing trends to be first on the bandwagon
  - o   Discover high-converting but low competition keywords that are easier to rank for
  - o   Use trend management to build a content calendar based on real numbers
  - o   Identify and target new demographics and niches

- Identify your top-performing content
  - o   Shine a spotlight on it by incorporating links into your advertising campaigns, newsletters, blog posts, etc.
  - o   Create more like it!

And this is just the tip of the data and analytics iceberg. There are many reasons why businesses don't invest in their analytics expertise. They think they aren't big enough for it, they don't realize how far technology has come, they think mastering it takes too much time or resources...

The truth is, every business can benefit from mastering data and analytics. It doesn't take a lot of time or resources to get started and the size of your business doesn't matter. If you're already successful, analytics will help keep you in the top spot. If you're growing or just starting out, analytics gives you a considerable edge to succeed.

Sounds too good to be true? Here's the catch: you have to be prepared to put the work in. Once you've mastered the tools, reports, insights and how to act on all of it, you need to be ready to stick with it. Analytics is not one-and-done. It has to be a regular, ongoing part of your strategy to stay on top of an ever-changing market.

But, if you're willing to put that work in, the payoff is more than worth it. So, are you ready to take FULL advantage of analytics?

Appendix

References

About author

Certifications

Other Books

Stay in touch

Chapter References:

https://datastudio.google.com

https://analytics.google.com

Google Analytics Support

https://support.google.com/analytics/?hl=en#topic=3544906

The data used in the analytics report is derived from three accounts:

- Montrealtips.com
- Google Demo Account
- Google Merchandise Store

Google Search Console: https://search.google.com/search-console/performance/search-analytics

Google AdWords: Google Ads - https://ads.google.com/intl/en_ca/home/

Keyword Planner - Google Ads:
https://ads.google.com/intl/en_ca/home/tools/keyword-planner/

Google Trends: https://trends.google.com/trends/

A big thank you for MOZ – MOZ.com for inspiring me to take the digital marketing route, and my thought process.

About the Author

Tarek Riman Bio

As Founder of Cap.TaiM, a full-service digital marketing agency, I have worked with 300+ agencies, SMBs and Fortune 500s, and hold 30+ certifications in digital marketing, including AdWords, Analytics, Bing, HubSpot, Woorank, Facebook & Hootsuite.

I am passionate about growing businesses and organizations through the strategic use of digital marketing tools, technology and data. I have great respect for the power of digital and believe we are living in a truly exciting time where individuals and organizations at all levels can harness that power to do great things. My mission is to show the world what we're capable of with a little understanding and a commitment to learning, trying, analyzing and trying again.

In pursuing this mission, I also founded Montrealtips.com, with proceeds going to the UN Refugee Agency, Montreal Children's Hospital and other causes, and am also involved with NGOs & charities in Canada & worldwide.

I am the international bestselling author of "The Camino Within", "The Secret to Capitalizing on Analytics" and "The SEO Way", and am a regular contributor to the Huffington Post, Thrive Global & Social Media Today. My fourth book, "The Digital Way", is scheduled to be released on May 20th, 2020.

As a speaker, workshop leader and university instructor, I teach and speak on topics such as Analytics for Businesses, SEO/SEM, Digital Marketing, WordPress, and Content Marketing.

Tarek Riman's Digital Certifications

Google AdWords Certifications

- Google Advanced Search

- Advertising Fundamentals

- Mobile Advertising

- Video Advertising

- Shopping Advertising

- Display Advertising

- Accredited Bing Ads Professional

- Google Tag Manager

- DoubleClick Rich Media

Google Analytics Certifications

- Google Analytics Certified Individual

- Digital Analytics Fundamentals

- Platform Principles

- Ecommerce Analytics

- Mobile App Analytics

- Advanced Google Analytics

- Google Analytics for Beginners

- Google Mobile Site

- Google Digital Sales

Facebook Certifications

- Targeting: Core Audiences Certification

- FB & Instagram Certification

- Promote Your Business from Your FB Page Certification

- Ad Auction & Delivery Overview

- Extend Your Campaign's Reach with Audience Network

Other Certifications

- Google Wildfire

- Woorank | Certified Marketing Partner

- Hootsuite Certified Professional

- HubSpot | Inbound Marketing Certified

- SEMrush SEO Certified

The Camino Within

A motivational book by Tarek Riman

Learn more about Tarek Through His First Book, The Camino Within

The Camino Within summary:

Have you ever felt that what you do is a reflection of what you've been taught and not a true reflection of who you are?

Have you ever felt that you've fast-forwarded through life, or have lived it on autopilot, just doing what's expected of you?

If you were to leave all your successes and possessions behind to explore beyond your comfort zone, what would you find?

Perhaps most importantly, what can you do today to become more alive in all your tomorrows?

Trek along with Tarek on his pilgrimage of physical and emotional endurance, of blistered feet and broken bikes, of the meeting of unlikely souls, and the generosity of some inspiring people he met along the way.

In The Camino Within, Tarek Riman takes you on an adventure through 500 miles of the Camino de Santiago, leading you to many insightful revelations he picked up along the way and brought home with him to stay.

Tarek will inspire you to intentionally and actively reflect on the stories you tell yourself, so that you can take your own personal Camino Within. He did this work by literally leaving everything behind: comfort, material possessions, technology, employment and important relationships! By breaking out of convention, he fueled his own personal growth, through which he provides key takeaways in every chapter to help inspire you to face your own personal challenges and aspirations. The Camino Within promises readers an engaging read that can give rise to adventures of the soul and a more meaningful life. This book will help you question your beliefs in order to understand, once and for all, if they are truly yours. It will help you see how powerful and cleansing such a journey can be, begin to uncover your own deep truths, and lead you to discover who you truly are.

To learn more about the book, check out thecaminowithin.com

The Secret to Capitalizing on Analytics

An Analytics book by Tarek Riman

The Secret to Capitalizing on Analytics' purpose is to help start-ups, students, beginners and entrepreneurs understand how to use data to optimize and improve their business and marketing strategies. All businesses today, no matter what their size, need to know how their website is performing. Without analytics, there is no way for a company to know how their website is performing in terms of attracting, informing and converting visitors.

In this book, you will learn how to get started with Google Analytics and how to set it up for optimal tracking. You will also learn to assess which marketing campaigns bring the best traffic to your website, which pages on your website are the most popular and how to extract information about your visitors. Information such as location, interests, age, behaviours and more so you can better understand your web traffic and capitalize on your marketing. You will also learn how to capitalize on the different trends and tools that are available.

Let's Stay in Touch

To stay updated on Tarek Riman's adventures, marketing for businesses or Montreal Tips, you can follow him on Instagram @taou, or check out his websites:

- The Camino Within Book Site: https://thecaminowithin.com
- The Secret to Capitalizing on Analytics Site: https://captaim.com/book
- The SEO Way book: https://captaim.com/seo/
- Email Tarek: triman@captaim.com
- Connect with Tarek Riman on LinkedIn: https://www.linkedin.com/in/tarekriman/
- Twitter: @tarekriman
- Instagram: @taou

Made in the USA
Monee, IL
11 September 2020